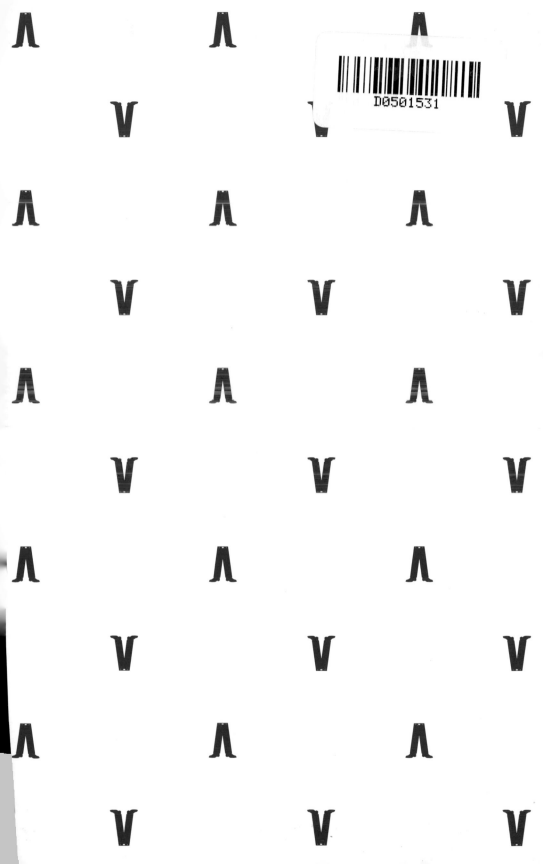

BALLS

A MEMOIR BY CHRIS EDWARDS

BALLS

IT TAKES SOME TO GET SOME

GREENLEAF
BOOK GROUP PRESS

BALLS is a work of nonfiction. The events and experiences I've written about are all true and have been recounted to the best of my ability. Some names and identifying characteristics have been changed in order to protect the privacy and anonymity of certain individuals. And so I don't get sued.

Published by Greenleaf Book Group Press
Austin, Texas
www.gbgpress.com

Distributed by Greenleaf Book Group

For ordering information or special discounts for bulk purchases, please contact Greenleaf Book Group at PO Box 91869, Austin, TX 78709, 512.891.6100.

Jacket design by DEUTSCH
Interior design and composition by Greenleaf Book Group

Cataloging-in-Publication data is available.

Print ISBN: 978-1-62634-325-2

eBook ISBN: 978-1-62634-326-9

Part of the Tree Neutral® program, which offsets the number of trees consumed in the production and printing of this book by taking proactive steps, such as planting trees in direct proportion to the number of trees used: www.treeneutral.com

Printed in the United States of America on acid-free paper

16 17 18 19 20 21   10 9 8 7 6 5 4 3 2 1

First Edition

For my fam. Love you more.

I PEE, THEREFORE I AM

March 1, 2004

So I'm standing there, peeing at a urinal for the first time.

What makes my situation different from the rite of passage most guys experience is two things:

1. I'm thirty-four years old.

2. There's a man behind me, cheering me on.

To clarify point two, the man is a doctor, not a pervert.

He also made my penis.

"Aim down . . . and don't bend your knees," he says, sounding like a Little League coach. I hear the pride in his voice and wonder if it's his handiwork or me he's really proud of.

"Did you check underneath the stalls?" I ask Doc, paranoid. The men's room appeared to be empty, but you never know.

"Yes, yes," he assures, then squats down to actually check.

I was "stalling" at the urinal, but my confidence was in the toilet and for good reason.

It was the night before my flight home to Boston. I'd been in Nashville for thirteen days—three in a hospital room and ten in a hotel room, only the last few of which were catheter-free. I was peeing standing up all right, mostly all over the bathroom floor and myself.

What's a no-brainer for most guys was proving to be a major challenge for me due to a few factors that make my man-made urethra a bit different from theirs.

First, there's the opening, which is a bit larger in diameter. Creating just the right size involves trial and error. If it's too narrow, some of the pee might get trapped inside and potentially cause an infection. So Doc had erred on the wider side, which explained the showerhead effect I had going on. Then there's the inconsistency of flow and direction due to post-surgical swelling. This was the reason my pee was shooting out at a forty-five-degree angle, forcing me to stand a full foot left of the bowl in order to get even close to hitting it. Finally there's the shape. Instead of being straight, the extended part of my urethra resembles the letter U—kind of like the pipe under a sink. Whenever I peed, some always collected in a "reservoir," which is why every time I'd think I was done and zip up, I'd get a warm sensation running down my leg.

I could deal with this in the privacy of my hotel bathroom, but as I packed my suitcase, I decided there was no way in hell I was ready to attempt to pee in a public restroom, let alone out in the open at a urinal.

Doc must have sensed my apprehension because just then my phone rang. "Heeeey, Chris. I've been thinking about your peeing. I want you to use the urinal before you go. And I want to be there when you do. Meet me at the bar in your hotel for a drink. I'll be there in ten minutes."

Filled with dread, I finished packing and took the elevator down to the lobby bar where my doctor sat, sipping a martini. I chased a vodka soda with two tall glasses of water and, armed with a full bladder and a clear view of the men's room door, psyched myself up. Once the only guy I saw go in had come out, I made my move. Doc followed a few paces behind me and waited by the sinks as I took my place on urinal row. Which brings me back to where I started and . . .

I have to say it was one of the most liberating experiences of my life.

No longer boxed in by a stall, it felt strange—almost like I was peeing outdoors. No more trying to balance myself to avoid touching the seat. Just unzip, whip it out, and go. The curved sides of the urinal also made it much safer to use than the toilet. No muss, no fuss, no worries about spraying guys next to me and getting my ass kicked.

On the flight back to Boston, I began making a mental bucket list of all the "guy things" I wanted to do now that I could pee standing up. Number one on the list: Write my name in the snow. It was the beginning of March; there was still time. My visualization of yellow letters on a fluffy white canvas was interrupted by the urge to pee followed by the joyous realization that I'd never have to squat in a godforsaken airplane lavatory again. The less time spent in those hellholes, the better. But thanks to my aiming difficulties and a bout of turbulence, I actually ended up spending twice as long in this one cleaning up the mess I made. Write my name in the snow? Yeah, right. I couldn't even hit the bowl—never mind forming actual letters.

Over the next few months, nobody's bathroom was safe. The direction of my pee was becoming more erratic. I walked around mentally assigning a degree of difficulty—from 1 to 10—to every toilet bowl I encountered: the smaller and rounder, the higher the degree. The things I had feared the most—urinals—were now my saviors; but still there were times when even they betrayed me, like that fateful night at the Loews Theater.

The movie had just let out. My friend Price waited in the lobby while I followed the throng of guys filing into the men's room. I took my place in line, praying that when my turn came up, one of the urinals would be free. Usually they rotated more frequently than the stalls, so I felt the odds were in my favor. But what opened up was the worst possible outcome: the center stall in a row of five. I froze, hoping the slight delay would give me another shot at a urinal, but the guy behind me helpfully pointed out the now wide-open metal door. I had no choice but to go in, unzip, and concentrate.

My pee actually squirted up and hit the wall in front of me. Then, as if defying all laws of physics, it veered right at a hard downward angle, shooting under the partition and into the next stall. I quickly adjusted my aim to counteract this directional disaster but overcompensated. My pee made a sharp left under the stall on the other side. I was certain any moment now, one or both of my neighbors were going to bust down my stall door with a pee-covered shoe and beat me with it. At the very least I expected a string of swear words to be hurled my way. But nobody yelled. And nobody tried to break in. Still, I stayed in that stall a good ten minutes, waiting out the crowd before making my exit.

I spotted Price where I'd left her. She looked concerned.

"Is everything okay?"

"Just keep walking."

The next morning I called Doc and recounted the "incident."

He laughed and then assured me he could fix my problem by making the urethral opening smaller. "One stitch should do it," he said.

Back to Music City I went—straight to Doc's office, where he put a stitch at the opening of the urethra. Afterward, I drank a bottle of water and we waited. And waited. And when I finally felt the urge, my pee . . . came out sideways.

This was not good.

"I need time to think," Doc said. "Let's go get a drink."

We found a dive bar off West End Avenue. Three-quarters of the way through my Diet Coke, I had to "go."

"I'll stay here this time," Doc said chuckling. Good thing he did. The men's room was the size of a broom closet and the urinal the size of a salad bowl. No savior here. *Degree of difficulty: 9.5.*

I returned to the table to find my surgeon drawing on a cocktail napkin.

"It wasn't pretty," I said.

"I figured it out," he announced.

Doc showed me his sketch of the head of my penis and then drew in how he would create a drawstring with the sutures to pull the urethral opening tighter and make it smaller from all sides. It worked. That one adjustment gave me the ability to pee with sniper-like precision and the confidence that I could handle any men's room situation that came my way.

I knew then what I know now: My gender identity is not defined by what's between my legs. Still, this was truly a defining moment for me as a man. And while there was still a lot more I'd have to go through before I'd finally feel complete, it would be nothing compared to what I'd already endured.

ARE YOU TALKING TO *ME*?

Summer 1974

I came out to my grandmother when I was five. I just didn't know I was doing it.

Neither did she.

I can't tell you what Gram was wearing at the time, but I'm sure it was something fashionable, which likely meant one of her bell-bottom pantsuits and a wrap turban with some bright, crazy pattern on it. Her mother, my Great Gram, was the matriarch of our family and owned a summer cottage on Cape Cod that served as the hub of our extended family gatherings from July through August. Because Great Gram's house was a short walk to Old Silver Beach, it wasn't uncommon to find six or seven of my relatives' cars wedged in like a jigsaw puzzle on the front lawn (and by lawn I mean crabgrass). On this particular day, my parents' wood-paneled station wagon was wedged in among them. Gram had driven down with us, which always made the ninety-minute ride more fun, and as usual my older sister, Wendy, and I fought over who got to sit next to her. There was only room for three people in the backseat, so with Grampa up front with Dad, and Mom in the back holding my baby sister, Jill, that meant one of us was destined for isolation in the way back. Still, Gram kept us both entertained by playing "I Spy" or having us compete to see who could spot the most VW bugs. When we got bored of that she'd tell us stories that she'd make up on the spot or put her own twist on classics like "Ali Baba and the Forty Thieves." That one was my favorite.

Gram loved the beach and once she gathered up her necessities— aluminum folding beach chair, sticky bottles of suntan oils, and rubber swim cap dotted with plastic daisies to protect her frosted hair—she walked us down to Old Silver where we spent the whole day taking in the sun. With both sides of my family being Armenian, most of my relatives had dark hair, brown eyes, and olive skin like Gram's that tanned easily. Wendy and I fit the bill. But it was sunblock slather sessions for Jill, who was inexplicably born with light brown hair, blue eyes, and fair skin. (We'd later tell her she was adopted and that the pale Ukrainian man who delivered Mom and Dad's dry cleaning was her real father.)

After a full day at the beach, Wendy and I were back at Great Gram's house in our t-shirts and shorts, hair still wet from the outside shower. We sprawled out on the faded Oriental rug in the family room with our coloring books and crayons, while Gram repeatedly passed by us on her route from the kitchen to the dining room carrying platters of shish kebab, salad, and pilaf.

On her last pass she yelled, "Come on, girls, dinner's ready."

Wendy immediately sprang up and followed her to the table. I didn't flinch. I honestly didn't think she was talking to me. Soon Gram was back kneeling across from me at eye level.

"Didn't you hear me calling you?" she asked.

"No."

"I said, 'Come on, girls.'"

"I'm not a girl," I replied, insulted.

"Yes . . . you are," she said gently.

"No, I'm not. I'm a boy."

"No, you're not, sweetheart."

"Well, then I'm gonna be," I insisted.

"You can't, darling," she said, then smiled sympathetically and walked back into the kitchen.

I'll show her! I thought.

Since everything about me was boy-like—my clothes, my toys, my obsession with all superheroes except for Wonder Woman and her lame, invisible plane—I put my five-year-old brain to work and determined that the only thing lumping me in with the girls was my hair length. Girls had long hair; boys had short hair. So to clear up Gram's and anyone else's future confusion on this matter, as soon as we got back home from the Cape I told my mom I wanted my hair cut "like Daddy's."

Many moms would have said "no way" to such a request, but my mom wasn't too concerned with gender stereotypes. "Nano," as friends and family called her, may have been traditional when it came to family, but she was relatively hip as far as moms went. She had given up her career in nursing to stay home and raise three kids while my dad worked his way up the ladder in advertising. She was extremely involved in our school activities from kindergarten through high school and was known as the "fun mom" who would plan the best birthday parties and supply endless trays of snacks and candy whenever friends came over. She'd even let us watch scary movies, though usually to our own detriment. Seeing *Jaws* at age seven led to an entire summer on dry land. Forget swimming in the ocean; I wouldn't even go near a pool. What if the shark came up through the drain?

Mom wasn't—and still isn't—a big skirt or dress wearer, so she never put Wendy or me in anything particularly girly when we were little— only Jill, whose favorite colors were pink and purple. Wendy and I were both tomboys. For us it was OshKosh overalls in neutral colors, Levi's corduroys, and "alligator" shirts. So when I asked to get my hair cut short, Mom took me to the barbershop in the center of town. After that, sure enough, everyone outside my family started calling me a boy.

Problem solved.

See, Gram, that wasn't so hard.

It wasn't until the following summer that I realized I was lacking certain "equipment." Still sandy from the beach, Wendy and I were eating popsicles with our younger cousin Adam on Great Gram's back deck, a danger zone for bare feet. I was standing on my wet towel in an effort to avoid another painful splinter-removal session with Mom's sewing needle when Adam nudged me and said, "Watch this." He then turned his back, and a stream of what I thought was water came shooting out of his red swim trunks over the deck rail in a perfect arc.

I was in awe. "How'd you do that?" I asked. "Do you have a squirt gun in there?"

Wendy, seventeen months my senior and always ready to educate (she dropped the "there is no Santa Claus" bomb on me seconds after finding out the awful truth), fielded the question quickly and effortlessly in a "*could-you-be-any-dumber?*" tone.

"It's not a squirt gun. He's *peeing.*"

How was this possible? When I peed it went straight down *and* I had to sit.

"But how does he get it to go up like that?"

"Because he has a *pee-nis.*"

This answer only raised more questions in my mind: *What is a "penis" and how come I don't have one?* I was too embarrassed to ask and something told me I didn't want to know the answers, for fear they would only lead to more evidence that Gram and everyone else in my family was right: I wasn't a boy like I thought—not even with my short haircut. It was easier to talk myself into believing my penis hadn't grown yet than to face that possibility. So every night I prayed that my body would change into a boy's body. That I would grow a penis—whatever that was—and everyone would finally realize they were wrong for thinking I was a girl.

Well, my body changed all right. Just not in the way I'd hoped.

Puberty struck and it betrayed me in the worst possible ways I could imagine. First, two buds began to protrude from my formerly flat chest, so I wore extra layers of clothing to hide them from myself and everybody else. I couldn't think of anything more traumatizing than having to wear a bra, let alone shopping for one.

I couldn't have been more wrong.

It happened the summer after my twelfth birthday on a fittingly stormy summer night. My family now had our own cottage in Old Silver Beach Village, directly across the street from Great Gram's house. While Jill had her own room, Wendy and I shared the larger front bedroom with its wood-paneled walls, cooling cross-breeze, and "magic" closet that you could walk into, turn a corner, and wind up in my parents' bedroom. The house had only one bathroom, which was decorated in a nautical theme and centrally located at the top of the stairs. It was so small you could sit on the toilet, stretch your legs out, and rest your feet on the tub. The living area was divided into a family room where we'd watch TV and a sunroom where we kept all our toys and games along with a bright green folding card table, the one piece of furniture in the house that got the most use.

Wendy and I were babysitting Jill and our cousins Adam and Dana while our moms were out bowling. The five of us were at the card table embroiled in yet another never-ending game of Monopoly. Looking past our reflection in the darkness of the picture window, I could see the rain coming down sideways in the glow of the street lamp, the sound of thunder getting closer and closer. Since everyone was focused on the lopsided trade Wendy was trying to con Dana into, I decided it was a good time to run upstairs for a pee break. And that's when I saw it: the red splotch.

I froze, my mind flashing back to the movie I had been forced to watch with all the girls in my fifth-grade class. My first thought was, *This can't be happening. Wendy's older than me. She's supposed to get it first.*

My second thought was, *I'm doomed.*

A loud clap of thunder crashed as if to accentuate the horror of my situation, followed by playful screams from below. I didn't know what to do so I began frantically stuffing the crotch of my underwear with toilet paper, the escalating storm echoing my panic. I walked downstairs with the gait of someone who'd just ridden his first rodeo to find my sisters and cousins staring out the window as a lightning bolt struck the telephone pole across the street. The lights inside the house flickered. They all screamed in unison, more out of excitement than fear, while I sat there trancelike on the couch. Just then, my mom and her sister burst open the door, soaked from the rain. Sensing what was to come, Mom rushed to the kitchen to find a flashlight and some candles while Aunty Barbie headed for the sunroom. Within seconds, another bolt of lightning struck and the whole house and street went dark. More playful screaming like what you'd hear on a roller coaster filled the room, only to be drowned out by uncontrollable sobbing. My aunt followed that particular sound to the couch and, after whacking her shin on the coffee table, felt her way to my shoulder and put her arm around me. "It's okay, don't be scared, Jilly."

"I'm over here!" Jill shouted from across the room. The surprise in Aunty's voice when she realized it was the twelve-year-old, not the nine-year-old, that she was consoling only made me feel worse. I wanted everyone gone so I could talk to my mom privately. Once she came in with the flashlight and began lighting candles, I took one up to my bedroom and waited for everyone to leave. When I finally heard the front door shut, I stood at the top of the stairs and called for her. Halfway up, she saw me looking down at her in tears.

"What's wrong?" she said, seemingly annoyed that her twelve-year-old was afraid of the dark.

"I got my period," I eked out. "What do I do?"

Mom seemed just as caught off guard as I was. She too expected Wendy would go first. She ushered me into the bathroom and looked inside my underwear to make sure. Her face softened and then she disappeared to the linen closet while I stood there helpless, looking through the crack in the doorway as Wendy and Jill hovered outside it trying to find out what was going on. Soon Mom returned with some maxi pads and a fresh pair of underwear and closed the door behind her. I couldn't speak. I knew my mom was talking, but I couldn't hear what she was saying over the sound of my whole world crashing down on me. I climbed into bed with what felt like a diaper between my legs and cried myself to sleep, quietly so my sister wouldn't hear.

In one night, any hope I had left of being the boy I knew I was evaporated. No matter how much I prayed, I was stuck with this body—stuck being a girl. And I knew things were only going to get worse. I saw a future filled with degradation: bleeding "down there" five days a month for the rest of my life, the public humiliation of buying tampons and pads and—oh God—bringing them to school with me!

Plus it was only a matter of time before those buds on my chest would no longer be hideable. The design on the front of every concert t-shirt I owned would soon be ruined by two protrusions held in place by beige lycra with a pink rosebud, and straps that would show through the paper-thin cotton. *Everyone* would be able to tell and would make fun of me. It was a life sentence of misery without parole. And it changed my whole personality.

From that moment on, I was no longer the fun-loving kid I used to be. My sense of humor went from good-natured to sarcastic. I was angry all the time, snapping at everybody for everything. Well, everybody at home that is. At school and with friends I put on an act and pretended like everything was fine. But as soon as I walked into the house, I took out all my anger and frustration on my family. I was bitter, envious of my sisters who were born "normal" and living carefree lives. I remember one Saturday walking into the family room to find nine-year-old Jill in her frilly pink and purple dress sitting peacefully at the coffee table watching a cartoon and eating a cupcake. A feeling of rage washed over me and I walked right over and punched her in the arm as hard as I could. She stared at me in confusion and started bawling. Tears welled up in my eyes as I realized what I'd just done. It wasn't my sister's fault I was the way I was. I hugged her and said I was sorry, but remained haunted by my action. As the middle child, I had always been the peacekeeper in the family. The one who quelled arguments and fights or prevented them from happening. Now I was the one starting them.

My dad was the first one to call me out on my behavior. Weeknights and weekends, I spent more time with him than my sisters did, probably because I was more interested in washing the car, throwing a softball around, and learning about all the different things a can of WD-40 could fix. After one of my outbursts, he kept me from stomping out of the family room and sat me down for a talk.

"Kris, you used to be so easygoing—the calm one in the family. What's wrong?"

"Well, how would you like it if *you* had to live the rest of your life as a girl?"

That's what I wanted to say. But I was afraid. I knew what I felt was "wrong," and if I said it out loud, there'd be no taking it back. Besides, what would be the point? There was nothing I could do about it anyway.

So I slunk deeper into the maroon leather sectional, looked down at my lap, and answered my father the same way almost any twelve-year-old kid would when asked that question: "I dunno."

What I did know was that I was attracted to girls so I thought I must be gay, and that was truly horrifying. This was the early 80s. There was nobody gay at my school. Well, there were people I suspected (I'm sure some suspected me), and many who probably were, but no one who ever publicly admitted to it. There weren't even any celebrities that were "out." George Michael was still in the closet, for god's sake, and those were the Wham! years. He was bopping around onstage in white Capri pants singing, "Wake me up before you go-go," and girls everywhere actually believed they had a chance.

I'd heard the word "gay" a million times. It was a derogatory way to describe something weird or odd or queer. I knew it really meant boys who "liked" boys. Girls who "liked" girls were lesbians but could also be called gay. Back then, saying something or someone was "so gay" was socially acceptable, so no one thought twice about it. Somehow "gay" evolved into "gay-bone" which everyone thought was a riot, including my sisters who picked up the term. My parents even said it on occasion. Hearing my family use these words made me even more ashamed and scared to tell them how I felt. So I called things gay and gay-bone too, just to fit in. If I didn't, people might think *I* was gay, which was way worse than me just thinking it.

The problem was, when I looked up the word "gay" in the dictionary (yes, I was that thorough), all it said was someone who is attracted to the same sex. There was nothing in the definition about feeling like you're in the wrong body or wanting to become the opposite sex. Same with the word "lesbian." So I figured I must be a freak, and there was no way I was ever going to tell anyone how I really felt inside—certainly not my family. I was too afraid, especially now that my mom was becoming more adamant about me wearing skirts and dresses to church. Wendy had grown out of the tomboy phase, and I guess Mom expected I would too. Instead I clung on to it for dear life. Maybe she was embarrassed by the fact that even in my early teens I was still being mistaken for a boy. Whatever the reason, I knew every Sunday morning there was going to be a battle about what I would wear. Sometimes I would win and leave the house in nice corduroys or the twill elastic-waist pants with the colored piping down the side that Mom had bought for me in the boys' department. Other times I'd end up in tears in my room, stuck having to put on the hideous skirt from the back of my closet that would make me feel like I was dressed in drag in front of my entire Sunday school class. My only saving grace was that none of those kids were from my town.

Unlike many Armenian families that tended to live in the blue-collar Watertown area of Massachusetts, my family lived in Wayland, a small, upper-middle-class Boston suburb. You can usually tell someone is "Armo" if their last name ends in "-ian," so being an Eskandarian, I easily identified the only two other Armenian families in the entire town. Those families were Catholic, not Protestant like us, so they went to St. Ann's in Wayland along with most of my other non-Armo friends. We, on the other hand, drove a half an hour to the First Armenian Church of Belmont where my mom went growing up. While the distant location of our church proved to be an advantage, overall my Armo heritage only made things worse. Not only did I feel out of place because my body was the wrong gender, but I looked out of place because of my olive skin and dark hair, which at this point was growing on my arms, legs, and upper lip way more than someone who was supposed to be a girl would've liked. Especially a girl starting junior high.

Still, I did my best to fit in. I shaved my legs. I bleached my mustache. I buried my feelings and made new friends. Like many girls my age, I covered my bedroom walls with posters of Rick Springfield. Not because I was in love with him like they were. Because I wanted to *be* him. Nonetheless, it served as good cover.

But it was going to take a lot more than that to be convincing as a girl, and the thought of ever having to wear a skirt or a dress in front of my friends and classmates made me physically ill. For that reason I dreaded formal events and did whatever I had to do to get out of them. A few of my new friends were Jewish and when a bat mitzvah or bar mitzvah invitation arrived in the mail, the pit that had taken up permanent residence in my stomach would get larger and I would shift into panic mode. I made up excuses and lies about why I couldn't go and then spent the month leading up to the event worrying about getting caught in my web of deceit. This went for chorus performances and school dances too.

I also declined all pool party invites, because putting on a bathing suit was even more traumatizing than wearing a skirt. Sleepover parties were crossed off my list after one girl noticed the pajama bottoms I was wearing had a fly. She announced to the whole group that I was wearing boys' pajamas, which led to an eruption of laughter and finger-pointing. The host came to my defense with an abrupt, "So what?" which put an end to their teasing; but I still wanted to crawl into my sleeping bag and zip myself inside.

Eventually my classmates caught onto my avoidance tactics and some became hell-bent on trapping me so they could see me in girls' clothes. One time, a few of the ringleaders convinced me to go out for field hockey and then waited until I was at tryouts to inform me that I'd have to play in a kilt. My solution: I played like crap and then justified quitting because I wasn't good at it. One birthday girl told everyone not to tell me her party was a pool party. She then called me up the night before to confirm I was coming and nonchalantly added, "Oh, and bring your bathing suit." Ugh! She got me.

My impending humiliation had me tossing and turning in bed until finally I gave up and crept downstairs, knowing I'd find my dad in his big black leather chair watching the eleven o'clock news. He was the one I always turned to for advice. Coming home in his business suits from a world where serious matters were discussed and analyzed, he always seemed to have the answers, or could easily come up with solutions to my problems. He heard me before he saw me.

"Kris, you scared me. What are you doing still up?"

"I can't sleep," I said.

He picked up the briefcase he'd been using as a lap desk and moved it aside so I could take its place. Sitting there, staring down at his loafers that I'd secretly try on when he wasn't home, I admitted I was embarrassed to wear a bathing suit and didn't want to go to the party. It was the most I'd ever said to anyone about how I felt. He told me everyone my age had something to be embarrassed about and confided that when he was growing up, he always had hairy legs and never liked to wear shorts. His anecdote didn't help solve my problem, but Mother Nature did: The day of the pool party it was pouring rain.

Then there were the dreaded make-out parties. I was constantly trying to avoid those too, conveniently disappearing when an impromptu game of spin-the-bottle broke out, always choosing "dare" to avoid having to answer questions about how far I'd gone or who I had a crush on. The peer pressure had me in a constant state of anxiety that regularly led me to the nurse's office with inexplicable nausea. My mom and the school nurse determined it must be motion sickness from riding the bus. While I was prone to getting carsick, I knew it was more than that. But I wasn't about to share my theory.

By the end of eighth grade I finally gave in and went to "The Last Dance" in a pink and white dress that my mom was thrilled to buy me. I felt totally ridiculous in it, and expected to be made fun of, but everyone told me how pretty I looked. And so, at age fourteen while dancing to "Straight from the Heart" by Bryan Adams, I had my first kiss. It was with the cutest guy in my class. Very good kisser. Soft lips. I remember for that brief moment going home happy—happy I'd gotten that milestone over with and seemed to be able to pass for a girl. I went to bed praying that from now on I would be attracted to boys and learn to like being the gender my body was born into.

Again, I was asking God to change me—this time on the inside, not the outside. Again, my prayers went unanswered.

Every morning I woke up still attracted to girls and still hating what I saw in the mirror. It was time to face the reality that in this movie called "My Life" I was stuck playing the role of "girl." I resolved to make the best of it and hone my acting skills. While it felt totally unnatural to me and keeping up appearances only added to my internal stress, I felt I had to do it to fit in. In high school when my friends talked about guys, I joined in the conversation. I'd say I had a major crush on someone clearly unattainable, like the good-looking senior football star with the hot girlfriend, and hope that would explain my lack of interest in other guys.

I continued to shop in the boys' department—I couldn't walk past it without the Ralph Lauren section drawing me in like a magnetic force field—but I also expanded my repertoire and began buying more girls' clothes. I was playing a role and I needed a better costume to be believable. I even let my mom talk me into getting my ears pierced. I think she thought it might help people stop mistaking me for a boy, which is why I agreed to do it. But, as soon as the gray plastic gun fired the first gold stud, I knew it was a mistake. While Wendy was choosing all kinds of earrings to take home, I sat on the mall bench with pangs of regret, which only got worse when I got home and saw myself in the mirror. I came downstairs the next day, minus the studs, hoping no one would notice, but Mom homed in on my naked lobes immediately and told me to put them back in before the holes closed. I had to think fast.

"Oh, they were hurting, so I just took them out for a bit."

She didn't buy it, and I wore those damn things for the prescribed six to eight weeks until the holes were permanently open. From then on, I wore earrings only if I had to dress up. Like for the one major high school coming-of-age ritual I could not avoid: The Prom.

There I was at Priscilla's of Boston, surrounded by Mom, Gram, and Wendy, trying on creepy dresses in various shades of pastel and hating every minute of it. Chewing glass would've given me more pleasure. The only reason I even went to the stupid prom was because not going would've caused me more scrutiny than putting on a pink tea-length dress. So I accepted the role of "female prom date," and went with a friend who asked with very respectable lead time. He was the kid who hit puberty in fifth grade—"the big one" who towered over all the other boys. He was good-natured, funny, and got along with everyone. This included our limo-mates, one of whom had recently suffered some type of mental breakdown and nearly backed out at the last minute.

I was ready to back out myself after coming home from the salon and taking a good look at what had been done to my hair. I didn't know it was capable of achieving such heights and asked Wendy to try to tone it down as well as apply the minimal amount of makeup necessary to pull off this whole nightmare ensemble. I performed all the other lovely rituals too: wore the wrist corsage (at least for the first hour), posed for cheesy photos, and partook in the obligatory slow dance to our prom theme, "Almost Paradise." Yeah, "almost" is right. Looking around the dance floor in my pink poofy dress with shoes dyed to match, I envied all the guys in their simple black tuxes. They were everything I wasn't; everything I wanted to be.

MORTAL THOUGHTS

College Graduation, 1991

"So, what are you gonna do after you graduate?"

With four years of college coming to an end, I was asked that question over and over by family, friends, the cashier at the local liquor store . . . And every time I answered it, I lied.

I just assumed "kill myself" wasn't the response they were looking for.

But that was my plan all along. Well, since senior year in high school anyway.

I knew I couldn't continue pretending to be a girl much longer; keeping up my act was exhausting. And to what end? When I looked to the future, all that was in store for me was more misery. Well, except maybe for college. That was supposed to be a blast. Everyone expected me to go and I'd worked hard throughout high school to earn the right. I may not have had a say in what body I was stuck with or who I was inside, but grades? Those I could control. So I focused on my studies to distract me from my gender issue and it paid off: high honor roll fifteen out of sixteen terms, number nine in my class of 240, SATs . . . never mind those. But I played sports and was in a bunch of clubs so I had the well-rounded thing going for me. Throughout the entire application process I figured I'd get in somewhere that would make my parents proud, party it up for four years, and then kill myself after graduation.

The first part of the plan was no problem: I got into Colgate University, which had a great academic reputation and happened to be ranked the number one party school in the US. I graduated in 1991 with a major in psychology and a minor in keg stands.

The killing myself part, however, was proving to be much more elusive. Certainly not because I was happy. I was back living with my parents under their roof and "their rules" while working as a freelance production assistant (aka "PA") on TV commercial shoots, which meant 6:00 a.m. call times, fourteen-hour days, and squat for pay. You'd think all this would've hastened my motivation. But instead I just kept delaying what I deemed to be the inevitable. Every night after the usual round of tears, I lay in my childhood bed wondering how I would do it.

Shoot myself? No way. Getting my hands on a gun would be too complicated, and even if I had one, I didn't think I could bring myself to pull the trigger.

Leave the car running in the garage? No guarantees. I could wind up brain-dead, not dead-dead.

Slitting my wrists was an option. I could contain the blood by being in the bathtub like in all the movies. But I hated my body. The last thing I wanted was to be discovered naked. I guess I could keep my clothes on . . . No. That would be weird.

Overdose? Yes, that was probably the best way, but on what? There was nothing in the house stronger than NyQuil, and like most of the condiments in my parents' refrigerator, that too had expired.

Months went by and I found myself still alive. I'd be behind the wheel staring at that solid yellow line and imagine suddenly swerving into oncoming traffic, then rule it out for fear of hurting someone else. Since I was apparently too scared to actively take my own life, I drove around without a seatbelt on, hoping for someone to hit me. And I was hit. Twice. But both times the car was parked and I wasn't in it.

Too miserable to live and too afraid to die, I somehow mustered up the courage to call my closest friend, Jess, who coincidentally was also the girl I hoped to marry one day. I'd met her my junior year at Colgate. She was a freshman and joined the rugby team I was on that spring.

Five-foot six, blonde, and blue-eyed, she had classic girl-next-door looks and was the nicest person I'd ever met. We all used to make fun of her for saying "sorry" all the time despite never being at fault for anything. She had the same sense of humor I did and a smile that made me melt. I began looking forward to practice simply because I knew she would be there.

We became fast friends and started hanging out outside of rugby. I would deliver pizza to her at study group, and she would drag me out of the library and into The Jug, the easiest bar to get into if you were underage. She lived in the dorms and I lived in a great house off campus with three roommates, so she ended up hanging at my place a lot. Jess didn't have a boyfriend but I knew it was only a matter of time. I was used to harboring crushes on girls only to suffer in silence when the inevitable boyfriend entered the picture, but it didn't stop me from fantasizing. Fantasy was all I had. All I knew. But with my reality now way too much to bear, I had to confide in someone. It was around 11:30 at night when I dialed her number.

Laying there in the dark, I told Jess everything. Through tears I described how ever since I was little I'd felt like a boy inside, and still did. That I was attracted to girls—specifically her—but that I knew I wasn't gay. That it was more than that. That I was in the wrong body. That I felt like I was living a lie and I just couldn't do it anymore.

She mostly just listened. While not having to face her made it easier, without seeing her face I couldn't tell what she was really thinking. I felt incredibly guilty about dumping all this on her at once. But when I was done talking she was extremely supportive and said she would be there for me. I wasn't sure if she meant as a friend or a love interest, but I didn't press for specifics. I was just happy she didn't call me a freak and hang up. What Jess was clear on was her worry for me. She encouraged me to speak with a professional—a doctor or therapist who could help me make sense of these feelings and figure out what to do next.

When I hung up the phone, I felt a mix of emotions: a sense of relief, the feeling that I wasn't alone, and at last, hope.

••

Jess was right. I needed to find a medical professional to talk to. But I had no idea how or where to begin finding the right person. This was 1992. I couldn't just Google "Doctors specializing in gender issues + MA" and get a list of names, phone numbers, and locations. There was no Google. Or Internet. I didn't even have a computer. So out of desperation I made an appointment with the only doctor I knew: my pediatrician.

It wasn't until I was sitting in "the waiting room time forgot," surrounded by children aged nine months to thirteen years, that I realized at twenty-three how badly I would stick out. Too old to be a patient and too young to be a parent, I clearly did not belong in that room. I felt all eyes were on me and was fairly certain the little boy whispering to his mother was telling her I was really a man.

After what felt like a lifetime, a nurse called my name, guided me to an examination room, and before I even had a chance to sit down, curtly asked me the reason for my visit. Knowing I'd likely have to get through this step before actually being able to speak with my doctor, I'd spent the drive over figuring out how I would answer this question. What I didn't expect was that the door would be wide open to the reception area, offering me a view of four-year-old "Olivia" hopping spastically around in circles for what appeared to be my benefit.

"I need a referral to see a specialist." Vague, but true.

The nurse looked at me impatiently. "For what?"

I stared at her. "Depression." Again, not a lie but not enough to satisfy her.

"Well, what are you depressed about?" She clicked her pen.

"I'd rather wait to speak with the doctor about that. It's kind of a long story."

She looked at me for a beat, unclicked her pen, and mercifully opted not to press me any further. "She'll be right in."

A minute later my pediatrician appeared and abruptly closed the door behind her. She looked pretty much the same as I remembered:

relatively tall for a woman and somewhat stocky with short dark hair, olive complexion, and a thick accent I could never really place. Hungarian maybe? She had been our family doctor for the last ten years so she also knew both my sisters and my mom. She always seemed like she was in a rush, which was clearly the case today. This was not going to be a nurturing visit.

"So Kristin, you are depressed . . . what's going on?"

"I, um . . . I . . ." And I broke down.

With tears streaming down my face, I managed to tell her I had always felt like a man inside—ever since I was little. That I have only ever been attracted to women, and that I couldn't live this lie or this life anymore. She brushed off my concerns, telling me I was not a man, just a "masculine woman." I told her I had seen a British model named Tula on *The Maury Povich Show*, who was a male-to-female transsexual due to a chromosomal defect and asked her to please run a test on my chromosomes; I was certain that I was a man and the test would prove it. She again told me I was not a man and that even if I was, the surgery for female to males was not medically possible yet so there was nothing I could do about it. I pushed again for the chromosome test and she relented, reasserting I was just a masculine woman and "probably a lesbian." She gave me the name of a psychologist in the building, suggested I start meeting with her regularly, and then told me to call back in two weeks for the test results.

I walked my paperwork down the hall to set up an appointment with my new psychologist. While waiting for the receptionist, I glanced at the referral form and noticed my pediatrician had written a diagnosis for me: hirsutism. I had no idea what the word meant, so when I got home I looked it up:

> **hirsutism:** *(noun)* Excessive growth of hair of normal or
> abnormal distribution

Are you fucking kidding me? I may be hairy, but I'm not stupid. This gender issue of mine was not going to be cured with electrolysis.

For the next two weeks, I prayed the chromosome test would yield an explanation for why I felt the way I did. I needed there to be a biological reason to make it okay. So it wasn't my fault. So people wouldn't think I was insane. So my parents wouldn't blame themselves. When I called my pediatrician's office two weeks later, they put me right through to my doctor who was pleased to inform me that I was "perfectly normal—no genetic abnormalities whatsoever."

I wanted to throw up.

I asked her to print out a copy of my results and leave it for me at the desk. Part of me didn't trust her based on the "hairy" diagnosis, and the other part of me hoped there was some mistake. Maybe my new psychologist would have an answer. Surely she would listen to me and understand where I was coming from.

But once again, I found myself trying to be talked out of my feelings and discouraged from even considering gender reassignment.[1] Not only that, it seemed she knew even less about the subject than I did. At my first session, I mentioned I'd done some research at the library and found the phone numbers for two gender clinics in the US and one in Canada. I told her I was going to ask all three places to send me information, but was living at home and for obvious reasons didn't want giant envelopes to arrive for me marked "Center for Gender Reassignment." She suggested I have them sent care of her office and she would call me when they arrived. Finally, a helpful suggestion!

I came back a few weeks later to pick up the information packets and found the envelopes had all been opened.

Huh, interesting. Last I heard opening someone else's mail was a federal offense.

"Who opened these?" I asked.

---

1   I'll be using the terms "gender reassignment" and "gender reassignment surgery" (GRS) throughout the book because that's what it was called at the time. But this terminology has since been deemed inaccurate; it is not one's gender being reassigned with surgery but rather one's anatomical sex. So "sex reassignment" and "sex reassignment surgery" (SRS) are the more commonly used terms. Today, however, the preferred and more politically correct terminology is "gender affirmation surgery" or "gender confirmation surgery."

"I did," she said. "I thought I should read the material so we could discuss it."

I felt violated and left her office fuming. On the way home I tried to rationalize her taking liberties with my mail. I guess it would make our sessions more constructive if she had the same information I did. Still, she should've asked my permission. I had almost resolved to forgive her when I sat down to read everything and discovered she had also taken a yellow highlighter to every detail about surgery that could be deemed negative or risky. It became clear to me that she had her own agenda and was not someone I could trust. I needed to find a new therapist—someone who could be objective and had experience treating patients with gender identity issues—but I was back to having no idea where or how to find such a person. I tried researching. I even asked my mail-tampering psychologist if there was anyone she could refer me to, that's how desperate I was. But there was no one to be found.

So in spite of her blatant act of betrayal, our sessions continued, which actually ended up being a good thing. To her credit, she got me to open up to my family—a more important first step than resolving my gender issue itself. More than ever I needed their support, and as much as I knew they loved me, I still wasn't sure I was going to get it.

ALL IN THE FAMILY

June 7, 1992

Another typical Sunday dinner at my parents' house. Only this one would end up changing our family forever. With Jill back from college for the summer, Wendy in between apartments, and me not making enough money to rent a PO box let alone my own place, my parents had the treat of all three of us living back at home again. It was just like old times. The only thing different was my nickname. Instead of "Kre," I was now being called "Shtiny," or "Shtine" for short (pronounced like "shiny" or "shine," only with a "t"). Don't ask, just go with it.

The five of us were sitting around the kitchen table in our usual seats, eating chicken and pilaf, our traditional Sunday fare. Well, everyone else was eating. I was pushing the food around my plate, sick to my stomach as I tried to get up the nerve to tell them all my big secret. I thought it would be best for them to hear it at the same time so no one would be forced to keep it from the others, and selfishly I didn't want to have the conversation more than once. Rip the Band-Aid off, so to speak. I chose dinner, knowing we would all be together anyway. The last thing I wanted to do was call a family meeting and have everyone staring at me expectantly.

From the moment I sat down at the table, I tried to think of a way in. My psychologist advised that I break it to them in stages, that it would be easier for them to digest my revelation that way rather than to come right out and tell them my end goal—gender reassignment. A logical approach, yes, but how the hell do I bring it up? *"Wendy, will you please pass the rolls and from now on start referring to me as your brother?"* If I had been gay, I could've just said "I'm gay" and all of them would've known what that meant. But there was no vocabulary yet for what I was going through. Today, kids could say they were transgender and, most likely, thanks to the media and celebrities like Chaz Bono, Laverne Cox, and Caitlyn Jenner, their parents would know what they were talking about. Or at least have a vague idea. But back when I was going through this, "transgender" wasn't really a word yet. The only word out there was "transsexual," and it had only negative connotations thanks to movies that portrayed transsexual characters as deviants and serial killers.

Take *The Silence of the Lambs*, Oscar winner for best picture. Its villain, "Buffalo Bill," was a serial killer who, as Dr. Hannibal Lecter put it, "fancied himself a transsexual." Having been rejected from a well-reputed gender clinic, he went on a killing spree, removing the skin from his female victims to sew himself his own female body. Lovely. I saw that movie senior year in college. I was supposed to go to a party afterward but went directly home instead.

Did the lambs stop screaming? No they did not.

Then came *The Crying Game*. When I saw it, I had no idea what it was about. Nobody would talk about the storyline for fear of giving away the "big surprise." They'd say, "Just go see it. You won't believe the surprise." Even the movie trailers simply said, "Don't ruin the surprise." Well, **spoiler alert,** "she" has a penis and it does not go over well with her male love interest, who, upon discovering said surprise, repeatedly pukes.

Great.

Not even comedies were safe. I went to see *Ace Ventura: Pet Detective* a few months later. I was laughing from the beginning of the movie right up until **spoiler alert** Ace figured out that detective Lois Einhorn, whom he had just made out with, was actually a man. To add to the hilarity, he then used a plunger on his mouth to induce vomiting while the theme song from *The Crying Game* played in the background. I felt the urge to vomit but for a different reason.

Meanwhile, television talk shows that sensationalized "real life" transsexuals weren't helping matters either. Their endgame wasn't to educate and inform the audience. It was to exploit their guests, most of whom were male to female and unable to "pass" as women in society's eyes, causing many viewers to label them as "men in drag" or worse, "freaks."

All of this is what everyone I knew would have as a frame of reference. It's what made me so scared to tell my family what was going on inside my head. I was afraid they'd look at me like *I* was a freak. Using the word transsexual to describe myself would not only frighten them but also lead straight to the surgery topic, which is what I was trying to avoid.

To make matters worse, I was struggling with the concept of gender identity myself. I had no idea where or how to begin to explain something so intrinsic to my being—something my whole family took for granted because their gender identities matched the bodies they were born with. My stomach was in knots as I listened to the chatter going on around me. Mom, Dad, and my sisters didn't seem to have a care in the world, and I was about to change all that. I caught my pained expression in the glass tabletop and almost began to cry.

At one point there was a lull and I opened my mouth to speak, still not sure what words were going to come out. I was cut off by a "Holy Moley" sighting, which prompted my dad to fling open the sliding glass door to the deck and shout obscenities at the giant mole that made its home in our backyard. He appeared only on Sundays, hence the name Holy Moley or "Holy" for short, and only during dinner when we were seated by the windows. Dad was convinced Holy was taunting us. Normally I found this entertaining. Not tonight.

I was running out of time. Instead of sitting back down, Dad took his plate to the sink and left the kitchen just as Jill was finishing a story she thought was hilarious. Paralyzed by my own anxiety, I didn't register a word she was saying, so when the punch line came and I was the only one at the table not laughing, she turned to me and jokingly said, "Oh, Shtiny, what's your problem?"

And that became my opening . . . for another one of my patented breakdowns.

Nobody knew what was going on. Jill held my hand and over the sound of my own sobbing I heard Mom say to Wendy, "Get Dad." When Wendy returned with my father, I was still crying hysterically, using my free hand to cover my face because I couldn't bear to look anyone in the eye. When I finally composed myself, I admitted to my family that I'd been depressed for years, had repeatedly thought about killing myself, and had been secretly going to therapy for the last three months. My hope was that they'd be so relieved I didn't commit suicide that whatever I told them next wouldn't seem so bad. I gave it a moment or two to sink in, wiped my nose with my shirtsleeve, and came clean.

Through tears, I told them that as far back as I could remember I had always felt I was a boy—even when I was five years old. I explained that that was why growing up I played with superheroes, cars, and action figures. Why I wore my hair short. Why I refused to wear skirts or dresses and always wore layers of clothing over my bathing suit. I told them I have only ever been attracted to girls. That in my dreams I was always male. That every time I looked in the mirror, what I saw didn't match up with who I felt I was inside. Finally, I admitted my feelings for Jess and told them she was the only one who knew any of this and had convinced me to get help. I didn't mention anything about surgery. I thought that was enough to dump on them in one sitting.

They listened intently. All of them were crying—even my dad, which was something I had witnessed only two other times in my life, both of them funerals. Jill never let go of my hand except to give me a napkin to wipe my nose, which had been running uncontrollably. It was Wendy who first broke the silence, trying to make sense of everything she'd just heard.

"So . . . you're gay?" Everyone kind of nodded and looked at me reassuringly as if to say, *it's okay, you can say it.*

I had a feeling this would happen; if I said I was attracted to girls, that would be the piece they would latch onto because being gay was something they understood. And perhaps something they suspected I was all along.

"No, I'm not gay," I said. "I mean, I'm attracted to girls, but I'm not gay. I'm in the wrong body."

Now everyone really looked confused, especially my mom, who in a well-meaning attempt to problem-solve, volunteered to sign us both up for the gym. "Maybe if you lost a few pounds and toned up, you'd feel better about your body. I'll go with you. We'll do it together."

My sisters looked at her like she was crazy. I appreciated Mom's sweet gesture and willingness to help but was getting more and more worried I wouldn't be able to explain this any more clearly without bringing up surgery. I was just about to "go there" when Dad stepped in and tried to make me feel better by explaining to me that gender is defined on a continuum.

"Kris, there is no black or white when it comes to male or female," he said. "There are effeminate males and masculine females, and you fall somewhere on the latter end of the spectrum."

I listened, wondering if he'd secretly had a talk with my pediatrician, but I didn't argue. I'd been processing this information my whole life. They were all hearing it now for the first time. I wiped my eyes and took in their faces. They all seemed to be wearing expressions of sadness and concern laced with confusion and what I took to be a hint of fear. I felt guilty for dropping this on them. Gay was one thing—*this* was way more than they bargained for.

Nonetheless, when all was said and done, there were lots of hugs and promises that they would be there for me and that we would get through this together as a family. Jill said, "I'd rather have you as a brother than not at all," which made me feel she'd read between the lines and truly understood that those were basically the only possible outcomes. Whether everyone else made that leap with her, I wasn't certain, but it was a great first step and their reactions were more than I'd hoped for. I felt a huge sense of relief to finally share this burden with them. I actually felt lighter.

The next day everything went back to normal.

And by that I mean it was as though the conversation never happened.

Days went by as I waited for someone in my family to just ask me how I was doing or feeling or if I wanted to talk—some form of acknowledgment that I didn't imagine the whole scene at the dinner table. But no one brought up the subject. After two weeks, when my disappointment was beginning to turn into anger, my dad asked me to go for a walk and gingerly broached the subject.

"So . . . how are you doing?"

"The same . . . thanks for asking."

"I've been wanting to ask, we all have, but we were afraid it would make you upset so we were waiting for you to bring it up again."

"Well, I was waiting for you guys to bring it up."

We both kind of laughed. This was starting to feel like an *ABC Afterschool Special.*

"So . . . did you meet with your doctor this week?" he asked. I was impressed. *Great way in, Dad.*

"Yeah, she was very proud of me for telling you guys and said keeping the dialogue open is really important. But she's still not validating any of my feelings about being a man. She treats me like I'm crazy even though there's a medical diagnosis for what I'm feeling."

"There is?"

"Yeah, gender dysphoria. I read about it in the information packets the gender clinics sent me."

I knew the definition by heart now.

gender dysphoria: *(noun)* A persistent unease with having the physical characteristics of one's gender, accompanied by strong identification with the opposite gender and a desire to live as or to become a member of the opposite gender.

The fact that there was an actual medical term that described what I had been feeling my entire life had completely blown my mind. It made me feel validated—relieved that I wasn't insane and that there were others who felt the same way I did. And now I hoped it would legitimize my "condition" in the eyes of my father. My dad is one of the smartest men I know—not just in the field of advertising but in all practical matters. He earned a degree in engineering at Villanova and worked for NASA before getting his MBA from Harvard. Knowing he thought like an engineer, I figured he would be drawn to a term that sounded scientific. I was right.

After I explained what gender dysphoria meant, he asked if he and Mom could read the literature the clinics had sent me. With my mom's background in nursing, I knew she'd be able to understand and translate all the medical stuff. The question was, were either of them ready to learn about and/or entertain the idea of surgery as a solution to my problem? I wasn't sure, but decided to roll the dice. When we got home I gathered the manila envelopes together with an elastic band and handed everything over, hoping it would prompt an open, productive dialogue. And then I waited. But not for long. The next day I found myself out for a walk with Dad again.

"Your mother and I read the material. Wow, all that surgery . . . that's a lot of pain and suffering to go through for results that aren't even that good. Seems like you agree that surgery isn't the way to go."

I looked at him cockeyed.

"Well, you highlighted all the negative parts, so we figured—"

"My *therapist* highlighted all that," I corrected. "She opened my mail."

"WHAT?" Apparently my dad was just as appalled as I had been when I discovered the crime.

"Yeah, as I told you yesterday, she clearly has her own opinion. But as far as I'm concerned, if I ever want to be happy, surgery is my only option."

There. I'd said it. We both stared straight ahead, avoiding eye contact, and continued walking.

Finally, Dad said, "Do you think you could just live with it . . . go on as you are now, keeping it inside, and just let this be your handicap?"

He said it with such hope in his voice, as though I could make it all go away with a simple "yes." *Sure, Dad—great idea!* Instead it was like a slap in the face. I thought back to my breakdown at the dinner table two weeks earlier—everything I had said about my depression and thoughts of suicide. I thought they had understood the severity of this issue. I thought I had made myself clear. I thought we were making progress.

"Dad, did you not hear me when I said I wanted to kill myself? This isn't something I can compartmentalize and put on a shelf. This is my identity. It's who I am every day. Imagine if you looked in the mirror every morning and saw a woman looking back at you. That all your friends, family, every person on the street, treated you like a woman. That when you went out to a client meeting, church, or formal event you had to put on a dress. Could you live with that? I've been doing it for twenty-three years and I just can't do it anymore."

And then the tears came. Thankfully, we were only one house from our driveway. I felt his arm around my shoulder.

"We'll figure it out, honey."

Ugh, I hate when he calls me that.

"Your mother and I just want what's best for you. We want you to be happy. We *all* want you to be happy."

I had to remind myself that this was only our third conversation on the subject. That my parents were going to need some time to think through all of this. It was unfair of me to expect them to be okay with everything right out of the gate. I'd been living with my gender issue my whole life. For them it had only been two weeks. I needed to be patient. They had a lot of catching up to do.

I didn't know it then, but according to my friend who works as a family therapist specializing in gender identity, this dynamic is very common in families today. By the time kids come out as transgender, they know who they are and expect everyone else to just "get it and get on board"—they've waited long enough for their lives to start. On the flip side, parents, often shell-shocked by the news, need time to process it and don't understand why their child is making such a "rash" decision. It's important for both parties to understand where the other is coming from.

But at least my parents and I were united on one thing: the mail tamperer's offense, which ended up being my mom's way of broaching the subject with me.

"Shtine, I can't believe that bitch opened your mail," said the woman who took the liberty of opening all my college rejection letters before I got home from school.

"I know, Mom. I have to find someone else." I then changed the subject from my psychologist's transgression to the real issue at hand. "So what did you think about the stuff you read?"

"I don't know . . . That's a lot of surgery to go through and it doesn't sound like they've perfected a procedure for females to become males. It seems like they can do it going the other way because you're removing rather than adding. I don't think you'd be happy with the results. Are you sure you're not just gay?"

"Mom, this goes way beyond what sex I'm attracted to. Believe me, it would be a lot easier for me if that was all it was."

"So you're not doing this for Jess?"

"What? No!"

Since Jess was not a lesbian, my mom was hypothesizing that I was going to change my sex in order to get her to want to be with me. I assured her that was not the reason—I was doing this for myself, for my own well-being. And while I did love Jess and hoped she actually would end up wanting to be with me, deep down I knew I couldn't count on a twenty-year-old girl still in college to make that kind of commitment.

"All those times in your room late at night when I yelled at you to get off the phone. You were talking to her about this, weren't you?"

I nodded.

"I'm so sorry, Shtine. I had no idea."

I squeezed her hand. "I know, Mom, I know."

NO, I'M NOT JUST REALLY REALLY GAY

December 9, 1992

Six months after the "big reveal" to my family, I sat in the waiting room outside the office of Bet MacArthur, a clinical social worker recommended to me by the program director at one of the gender clinics I'd reached out to. She had a private practice in Cambridge, and, most importantly, years of experience treating patients with gender dysphoria. Thank God!

Five minutes early for my appointment, I could hear muffled voices coming from behind the closed door, one of them more agitated than the other. Ten minutes later, I'm still waiting and the voices don't seem to be winding down. This strikes me as odd. Aren't therapists usually pretty strict about time? On TV and in the movies, there's always a bell or something that goes off when time is up and the patient is abruptly interrupted in the middle of an epiphany only to be escorted out and told "same time next week."

A few minutes later the door finally opened and a male figure quickly stomped past me on his way down the narrow flight of rickety stairs. Standing in the now-open doorway, Bet smiled and invited me inside. She was in her late forties and exactly what I pictured a Cambridge therapist would look like: straight, shoulder-length brown hair, graying and parted in the middle, big round glasses, no makeup, wool turtleneck sweater, corduroy pants, sensible all-weather walking shoes . . . If I were a betting man I would have wagered fifty bucks that the old Subaru Outback parked in front of the building was registered in her name.

"Sorry about the delay," she said. "I don't usually run late with patients, but this one needed some extra attention today."

"No problem," I said, surveying the contents of the largely beige and brown room: one lumpy couch, two well-worn chairs, a side table in need of a good dusting, a generic glass pitcher half full of water, a small sleeve of tiny plastic cups, and a box of Kleenex. I wasn't sure where I was supposed to sit so I waited for her to sit down first. She just stood there, looking at me.

"Where should I sit?" I asked.

"Wherever you'd like."

Having been a psych major, I'm thinking she's going to analyze my selection. *If I choose the seat closest to the tissue box will she think I'm sad? If I choose the seat she usually sits in will she think I'm a control freak? Hmmm.* I opted for the seat on the couch directly opposite the big chair simply because that's what I thought made the most sense. We then proceeded to have a staring contest. *Why won't she just ask me a freaking question?* Again, the psych major in me assumed this was some kind of psychoanalytical trick. Whatever it was, it made me uncomfortable. But it didn't take long before my wish to be asked a question was granted. As it turned out, asking me questions was her way of *answering* all *my* questions.

> Me: So . . . where should we start?
> Bet: Where do you want to start?
> Me: I don't know. Wherever you think is best.
> Bet: Where do *you* think is best?

Oh my god, I wanted to throttle her. I needed someone to take the lead here, not play stupid mind games with me. I decided to give her my background first, thinking that would be easy and hopefully the questions would follow. I told her about my family dynamics, where I grew up and went to college, and by the time I got to the present I was on a roll. "Today, I'm living at home with my parents and working as a freelance production assistant while trying to get up the nerve to kill myself. I am tired of pretending to be a woman. I am a man trapped inside a woman's body and I can't take it anymore. Oh, I'm also in love with my best friend. There, that about covers it."

If Bet felt any sympathy or emotion, her expression didn't show it. She turned the conversation to gender, specifically asking what I thought the differences were between men and women. Something told me "pee-pees" and "va-jay-jays" was not the response she was looking for. She wasn't talking about external physical characteristics; she was talking about gender identity. What makes someone a man *inside*? What makes someone a woman? The answers seemed so obvious but, like that fateful night at the dinner table, I struggled to articulate them. It's something you just know; something most people take for granted.

I wasn't like most people.

I continued to meet with Bet twice a week, and she continued to ask me the same questions over and over again. Tired of talking in circles, I finally asked, "Are these trick questions you're asking me? How do I know I'm a man? I just do."

"Have you considered the possibility you might be a lesbian?" she asked.

I told her how, when I came out to my family, they initially thought and then hoped I was "just gay"—that maybe I was a butch lesbian—and that there had been a time when I wondered that too. I was thirteen and my friend from St. Louis who came to her grandparents' Cape house every summer invited me to go to Provincetown for the day with her family. I'd never been, but had heard that P-Town was "where all the gay people went for vacation." While we were walking around, I noticed a lot of stores with rainbow flags selling t-shirts and bumper stickers with the word "dyke" printed on them. I asked my friend what it meant. When she said "a really masculine lesbian" I immediately felt my stomach tighten. I knew I was only attracted to girls and I did dress like a boy—was even still mistaken for one quite a bit. *Oh my god. That's what I am: a dyke. That's what people are gonna call me.* I couldn't breathe.

Then my friend helpfully pointed out a few examples and I started to feel a little better. These were big burly women with crew cuts and what seemed to be a penchant for either the lumberjack or biker lifestyle. One of them even bore a striking resemblance to my industrial arts teacher . . . Okay, so maybe I'm not a dyke but just a "regular" lesbian? But that wasn't sitting right either. So I asked myself one simple question: *If being gay was "normal," would I be happy? Could I be happy?* The answer was no. Because it still wouldn't change the fact that every time I looked in the mirror I hated what I saw.

When I recounted that last part to Bet, I finally saw the hint of a smile.

The key to understanding gender dysphoria is realizing that sexual orientation and gender identity are two totally different and completely separate things. One isn't dependent on the other. This is where most of the initial confusion happens—for everybody. Even after sitting on Bet's couch for hours analyzing gender identity to death, I didn't truly get it until I attended my first female-to-male support group. There were five attendees including myself, all of us curiously under 5'5". The other guys were "ahead of me" in that they had already been living full-time as men and, judging by two pubescent mustaches and one attempt at a goatee, at least three of them had already begun testosterone injections. One member, who I'll call "Brian," was telling the group he used to be married when he was a woman and that since his divorce he's been living as a man while attending grad school.

I sat there thinking, *Wow. This dude had been married and ipso facto been having sex with a guy—gross.* It was something I could never imagine doing because to me, even though I was anatomically a woman, inside I was a man. Wanting to have sex with another man would mean I was gay. I was definitely not gay.

As it turns out, Brian was. He was going to go through the entire transition process—including surgery—to become a man, only to still be attracted to other men. When he told us all this, my first thought was, *Why bother? Just live your life as a woman, date all the guys you want, and society will deem you "normal."*

And that's when, as Oprah would say, I had my "aha moment." Brian's gender identity was completely separate from his sexual orientation. Like me, his gender identity was male, but while I was "straight" (attracted to women), he was "gay" (attracted to men). He still looked in the mirror and hated what he saw just like I did. The fact that he was still attracted to men had nothing to do with that.

Bottom line is, your gender identity has no bearing on whether you are gay or straight. Think of it this way: Sexual orientation is who you go to bed *with*; gender identity is who you go to bed *as*. That distinction is what really made it click for me.

But understanding it didn't make everything all better. I was still extremely depressed and crippled by the fear of what my future had in store for me. I couldn't focus on anything else.

When I relayed these symptoms to Bet, she suggested I consider an antidepressant and mentioned the relatively new drug, Prozac. I was adamantly opposed to the idea for a number of reasons. At the time, there was a stigma attached to the medication—to many people, taking it meant you were mentally unstable. I was depressed for sure but not unstable, and I didn't need that label attached to me on top of everything else. I also feared the pills would change my personality. I pictured myself with a stupid grin plastered on my face 24/7, laughing at lame jokes instead of rolling my eyes like I normally would. On top of that, I assumed any happiness I might feel while on Prozac would be chemically induced and therefore fake, rendering it impossible to tell if I was making real progress. Finally, to me, pill popping was a sign of weakness. It was only my eighth visit, and I wanted to try to cure my depression with good old-fashioned therapy before resorting to mind-altering drugs.

But four months later, after major bouts of insomnia and the inability to concentrate on anything but my gender conflict, I found myself in Bet's office asking her to tell me more about this wonder pill. She assured me it would not change my personality—that I wouldn't really notice when it kicked in—but that soon I would just start feeling better overall and life would go more smoothly. The main reason she thought it would benefit me was that it would help stop me from feeling "stuck" all the time—it would free up my mind and keep me from dwelling on things. I'd still feel the full range of emotions, including sadness, but I'd be able to move on from those feelings, focus on other things and be better able to problem-solve.

"Okay, I'm in," I said with new hope. Since clinical social workers are not licensed medical prescribers, Bet referred me to a psychiatrist who, after a one-hour evaluation, agreed Prozac would help me. I left his office with a prescription and directions to the nearest CVS.

"I got the goods!" I announced to my parents as I came home after work that Friday, shaking my bottle of pills. I was told to take one the same time every morning after breakfast. Since it was the weekend, I woke up later than usual and took my pill at around 11:00 a.m. It didn't strike me until Monday morning when I came downstairs ready to leave the house at 8:15 that to keep on the same schedule, my Prozac would be accompanying me to work.

"Wait!" Mom yelled, opening the kitchen cabinet that held all the cough syrup and aspirin. "Here, I'll dump out this bottle of Tylenol and you can put your pills inside."

"Mom, it's fine. I'll just keep it in my drawer."

Too late. The Tylenol capsules were already clacking and scattering all over the counter.

"No, no, no, this is better," she insisted.

"Jesus Christ, Nance!" my dad yelled. *Finally, the voice of reason.* "What if she forgets and takes a couple when she has a headache?"

What the what?

Dad turned to me. "Here, give me that bottle," Before I could blink, he'd snatched it out of my hand and grabbed a pen. "I'll just cross out the word 'Prozac' so you can't read it."

I stood there watching the two of them argue over the best way to conceal my new prescription-drug dependency, and instead of getting annoyed, I actually found myself smiling.

Hmmm . . . it's only been two days . . . could the Prozac be kicking in already?

No, but six weeks later I began noticing subtle differences that could only be attributed to the medication. Actually, other people noticed and pointed them out to me. They said I looked "refreshed" and "more relaxed." I realized then I had been sleeping better. When I went to bed at night, I was no longer lying there awake for hours stewing over my gender situation and imagining the worst. I'd still think about it—the issue didn't magically disappear—but like Bet promised, I was able to move on. Same thing during the day: My problem was still there, but I wasn't obsessing over it anymore. I was able to focus on other things. I started going out with friends again. Friends I had previously distanced myself from during my suicidal days so they wouldn't feel hurt or miss me when I was gone.

Things were looking up and my parents seemed relieved, especially when I told them I was thinking about moving out. A few months prior, three of my best friends from high school had rented an apartment in Cleveland Circle near Boston College and asked if I wanted to move in with them. They needed a fourth and to my family's surprise I declined. I just couldn't do it. Not in the state I was in. These friends were girls. I didn't want to be part of the whole "girls living together" mentality anymore—with siblings or roommates. It was bad enough I spent my high school and college years sharing a car with my sisters that, thanks to my Dad's clever wit, bore the license plate "GIRLS 3." I was officially done lumping myself into that category. I also didn't want to have to explain my whereabouts if I was at therapy or make excuses for why I was crying in my room.

Now here I was talking about getting an apartment with a friend. The difference was this friend was a guy.

Jim was one of my best friend's boyfriend's best friend. (Got that?) We had started hanging out in a group, mainly at parties when we were all home on breaks from college. He was a good guy, a bit quiet, but had a great sense of humor and was able to keep up with my friends and me when it came to beer chugging and movie quoting. When he started to ask me out separately, I knew where things were headed. I tried to politely dodge bullets and shield myself from advances. One time I even made my mom stand in the hallway to squelch a goodbye kiss that I sensed was in the works. Things were getting too close for comfort, and I was happy to escape back to Colgate for senior year. A week or two later I got a letter from Jim confessing his feelings for me and wanting to know where I stood. I felt I needed to be honest, but what could I tell him? *It's not you, it's me . . . I'm a guy*. I don't think so. I spent hours crafting my response, letting him know I didn't share those feelings but that I really valued his friendship. Cliché, I know, but it was the truth.

I didn't hear back from him.

When I came home after graduation we saw each other at a party. It was awkward at first, but over time things fell back to normal. We gradually began hanging out again, watching football, going to pubs, and shooting pool. We complemented each other nicely. He taught me how to shotgun a beer and play darts. I taught him the rules of 7, 11, or Doubles, and that wearing sweatpants out to dinner was unacceptable. When he started talking about wanting to move out of his apartment and finding a new place closer to where he worked, the opportunity seemed too perfect.

I ran my idea by him and his eyes lit up.

"Roommates, Jim. Nothing more."

"Don't flatter yourself," he said. "Are your parents gonna be okay with this?"

Why wouldn't they be? We're both guys. "Oh yeah, they're fine with it. They know we're just good friends."

While Jim was impressed with Mom and Dad's "progressive attitude," I was impressed with my own progress. Getting out of my parents' house and getting on with my life independently was a huge step forward. Looks like I wasn't "stuck" anymore.

WORKIN' IT

March 11, 1993

Sitting uncomfortably in the black leather and chrome guest chair inside Ron Lawner's office, I couldn't help but feel intimidated. Ron was the Chief Creative Officer at Arnold, one of the top ad agencies in Boston, and would eventually become the creative guiding force behind the award-winning "Drivers Wanted" campaign for Volkswagen. Right now he was interviewing me for the junior copywriter position that had just opened up. Poised behind a sleek desk in one of his signature black t-shirts (which probably cost more than my total income), he silently flipped through my "book" of spec ads, each one suddenly seeming lamer and lamer to me by the second. He chuckled at a TV spot I wrote for Safe Sun, a sunblock product I'd made up, which I thought was a good sign. But by the fourth ad in the campaign, he just turned the page. *Damn it! I knew I should've stopped at three.* The page turning got faster and faster until he finally closed the book and said, "Well, you've got a few good ideas in here. When do you want to start?"

"You mean I'm hired?"

He looked at me like, *"Duh."* Apparently I was the only one who thought there was a chance I wouldn't get the job. While I'd interned in the creative department at Arnold the summer before and was told I was a pretty good writer, what got me this interview was my connection to the agency's owner and CEO: my father.

I wasn't crazy about the idea of working at my dad's shop. The slightest whiff of nepotism made me uncomfortable. But after objectively evaluating all the agencies in town, I liked Arnold the best. Plus I didn't plan on working there very long. I was going to move away when I transitioned, so I just needed a job to last me the next year or two. And I knew I couldn't stick with my current job as a PA much longer. The early call times, long days, and lousy pay were necessary evils if you wanted to be a producer, but I was more interested in coming up with ideas for spots than figuring out how to make them within budget.

I had told my dad I wanted to go about this the right way; I was going to take creative concepts classes and put a book together just like every other aspiring copywriter. He agreed with my plan, adding that he wasn't going to have the company just create a job for me, and he didn't. Nine months later one finally opened up, and as I was accepting it, it suddenly occurred to me that despite my writing skills and all the time I spent putting my book together, there was a pretty good chance the only reason I got this job was because my last name was the same as the CEO's. Seeing that Eskandarian isn't all that common, it also struck me that it was highly likely everyone else at the agency would know I was related to "Big Ed" and, as a result, question my ability.

That night I asked Dad if he'd told Ron he had to hire me.

"I told Ron when a position for a junior writer opened up that I wanted him to consider you for the job—to meet with you and look at your book. After that, if he didn't think you had any talent, he didn't have to hire you."

"I doubt he would tell you your kid had no talent."

"Well, that's what I told him," he snapped.

Shit, now I was sounding ungrateful.

"Listen," he said more sympathetically, "because of me, you're gonna have to prove yourself—it goes with the territory. Just work twice as hard as everybody else. And don't complain. Once they see you've got talent, it won't be an issue."

I tried to keep that in mind when I showed up for work that first day, but the fear of being judged and not being able to measure up lingered in the back of my mind as I met my fellow creatives. There were forty in the department, ranging in age from early twenties to early fifties. Most people were friendly, but I did notice that many conversations came to a screeching halt when I approached. Did people honestly think I was going to run and tell my dad everything that happened around here? That Dad and I sat at the dinner table every Sunday going through the department list and making black marks next to anyone who said anything negative about the agency? Besides the ridiculousness of the idea, I couldn't see that there was even anything to complain about.

I got in before 9:00 a.m. because that's when Ron got in, but everyone else strolled in around 9:30. And you could come and go as you pleased, which was a new concept for me because as a PA, I had to report my whereabouts every five minutes. After a week of stopping by my department manager's office to tell her when I was leaving for lunch or stepping out to go to "an appointment" (therapy session with Bet), she finally said, "Kris, you don't have to check in every time you need to go somewhere. Just go. You can manage your own schedule." I immediately left the building to go buy a pack of gum. Just because I could.

Another bonus: Unlike the rest of the agency, as a creative you could wear whatever you wanted—a big reason I was drawn to this side of the business: No skirts required. While some creatives chose pajama bottoms and flip-flops, my androgynous wardrobe of jeans and Ralph Lauren button-downs became my uniform. You could also skateboard to meetings, play corn hole in the hallways, and at 4:00 p.m. sharp swing by Goransson's office for his infamous "rose martinis" made with gin and a splash of Chambord. Yeah, I'm liking this job.

I liked the Arnold culture even more. Every Friday was "Sunset Lounge," which meant beer, wine, and snacks for all three hundred employees at 5:00 p.m. In the summer you got every other Friday off. You also got your birthday off as well as a bunch of extra days around the holidays. And while this was hardly the era of *Mad Men*, our Christmas parties and summer outings could rival a few episodes. A source from Boston's renowned Bay Tower Room reported that the Arnold Christmas party of 1996 had the highest recorded bar tab in their history. The day after every party, you'd find out who won the "Lampshade Award." That year the decision was obvious—I just thank God it wasn't me.

Fun and games aside, what made Arnold so special was the bond that came from feeling both proud and lucky to be working there. We were a tight-knit bunch and for the most part, everyone treated each other with respect. It truly felt like we were a family—one that was led by a well-respected CEO who cared about each and every member.

Per that CEO's advice, I worked my ass off, taking all the jobs nobody wanted without complaint. My first real assignment was writing headlines for supermarket circulars and those plastic dividers at the registers that separate your groceries from the person's behind you: *No cash. No check. No problem.* Now that was a stellar piece of copy. When my mom first saw it in action at the grocery store, she held up the divider and announced to everyone in line, "My child wrote that!" Somehow that long, skinny piece of plastic managed to wedge its way into one of her grocery bags. She thought I would like it for my office.

Then there was the catchy line I wrote for the meat department: *No one can beat our meat.* I had included it among a list of other options as a joke, but the account person never caught it and the client ended up featuring it in a giant banner over the deli counter. Apparently a few customers got the joke and didn't think it was very funny. It was pulled down three days later. *Oops.*

After six months on the job, I graduated from a cube to an interior office, where Ron found me one night while "making his rounds" (i.e., popping into creatives' offices to see what they were working on or, according to my department mates, seeing who was still hard at work after 6:00 p.m. and who had gone home). His eyes focused on the wall to the left of my desk, where the back-to-school ads I had just brainstormed with my partner were hanging. Rough tissue layouts represented our best attempts at peddling Trapper Keepers and other school supplies for a local retailer, including another ad I had written for laughs, which Ron was now slowly reading out loud for dramatic effect.

"Is that a pencil in your pocket, or are you just excited for our back-to-school sale?"

"That one's a joke," I said, sheepishly.

"I like it. You could make a campaign out of it. You know, is that a ruler in your pocket? . . . A protractor in your pocket?"

Oh my god, this was amazing! Ron Lawner likes my idea and is concepting with me. "Really, you think so?"

"No."

He then smirked and sauntered out. Great, any points I earned for working past six were just nullified by my stupid "pencil in your pocket" line. I soon learned this was Ron's sense of humor and that he messed with everyone that way. Still, I was glad he never made his rounds while I was concepting the Blue Cross Blue Shield ad for the Braintree Hospital charity golf tournament. I'm not sure what he would have thought of *The one time you won't tense up seeing a doctor put on a glove.* The clients loved it, though, and soon the local healthcare provider became one of my main accounts. When it came to creative, they got "it" and my sense of humor.

Even better, on the agency side, so did the team's account manager and traffic manager. Beth and Mandy were my age and a blast to work with. Beth had a warm smile, a face full of freckles, and an Ann Taylor frequent shopper's card. She was by far the most professional of the three of us. Mandy had staggering blue eyes, long blonde hair that by three o'clock was usually pulled back in a ponytail, and a laugh that could be recognized from the other side of the floor. The three of us were inseparable.

But the one thing about having close female friends: The more time they spend with you, the easier it is for them to tell when something's wrong. So, when I came in one Monday after spending most of the weekend in tears, it didn't take long for Beth and Mandy to start probing. I wanted to tell them, but what was I going to say? *Well, guys, on Saturday the girl I've been in love with for the last three years informed me that she's in a relationship with someone, and the reason she hasn't been returning my calls for the past few months is because she knew I had feelings for her and didn't know how to break it to me. I was hoping she wouldn't date anyone until I had my gender reassignment surgery and then we could be together and get married.*

I was not ready to go there. "I don't want to talk about it" was all I could muster up.

I had managed to get through the first part of the weekend unscathed. My roommate, Jim, could tell I was upset; but guy friends don't pry when it comes to this sort of thing. I knew he'd wait for me to bring it up if I wanted to talk about it. When Sunday morning rolled around, though, and I still hadn't said anything, he finally caved and asked me if I was okay. I said yes, knowing he'd follow guy code and drop the subject—whether he believed me or not.

On Sunday afternoon I drove out to Wayland for family dinner. The last thing I wanted to do was have another breakdown at the table, so I put on my best face and decided to leave early so I could be alone with my misery. I was fine until I went to say goodbye to Dad, who was in the garage digging up a bucket and some sponges to wash my sister's car.

"You're leaving already?"

"Yeah, I got stuff to do."

"Is everything alright? You seem sad today."

You know those times when you're upset but you think you have your emotions under control, and then you call home and your mom or dad answers the phone and just hearing their voice makes you burst into tears? It was like that.

"Jess is seeing someone," I blurted out. He pulled me into a hug.

"Oh, I'm sorry. I know how you feel about her. But what did you think was gonna happen?"

I pulled away and looked at him, confused.

"Did you really think she would wait for you?"

Ouch.

It wasn't that I thought she would, more that I'd hoped she would. I'd naively made Jess part of my future, even though deep down inside I knew it was just a fantasy. In my dreams I was a man and I was married to her (and taller than her). Who was I kidding? She had her whole life ahead of her. She could have any guy she wanted. Why would she want to saddle herself with someone who required years of surgery to physically turn himself into one?

But I needed something to believe in, to keep me going, and that something was Jess—or more accurately, the dream of Jess. And now she was gone and I had nothing to hope for. The pain was constant. The Prozac helped me focus on my work, but in between meetings, the dull ache would return.

Beth asked me almost daily if I wanted to talk about anything. I told her there was something—something I wasn't ready to talk about yet—but when I was, she and Mandy would be the first ones I'd turn to. That time was coming soon; I knew it.

So did my therapist. Bet had finally confirmed my self-diagnosis: I was indeed transgender. Her official diagnosis was critical to me for a few reasons. First and most obvious, it validated what I'd known all along and gave me a major sense of relief; I was not crazy (as the previous two doctors would have had me believe). Second, it made my situation very real. This wasn't going away. I was going to change, and as a result my whole world was going to change. Lastly, it meant I had completed step one of the gender reassignment process (back then an official diagnosis was required if you wanted to have surgery). I could now begin socially transitioning whenever I was ready. But just because I was ready didn't mean my parents were.

A loving and supportive family is critical to a successful transition. Unfortunately it's something most trans kids do not have and a big reason why more than fifty percent of them will attempt suicide before their twentieth birthday.[2]

I was lucky. When I told my parents I wanted to change my gender they didn't shun me or kick me out of the house. But they did initially ask me to reconsider. My dad spoke for both of them, telling me they were worried I'd be worse off, that I wouldn't be able to pass, that I'd lose

2   Statistic found at http://www.yspp.org/about_suicide/statistics.htm.

my friends, that strangers would laugh at me on sight—that it would be harder for me to adjust and live a "normal" life than it already was.

And how could I blame them? What little information there was on this topic was mostly negative and, thanks to the mail tamperer, highlighted in yellow. There were no success stories they could look to for reassurance, and surgery to go from female to male was nowhere near where it is today. They were scared. And so was I. Not just because I was about to risk everything for a chance at finally being happy, but because my father, the man I'd always gone to for advice, was advising against it.

And for the first time in my life, I wasn't listening to him.

THE "HIT LIST"

Fall 1994

I may be transgender, but I'm also a Taurus—as stubborn as the day is long. So when Bet started questioning my plan to move out of state to undergo my transition, the bull reared its ugly head.

"What do you mean? Of course I have to move away."

"How come?" Bet asked. "Why can't you do it here, where you have a support network?"

I laughed sarcastically. "Are you living in Fantasyland?"

"Have you stopped to consider it?"

"No. I haven't considered it."

"Why not?"

"Because first of all, I'm not going to humiliate my family."

"Why do you think your family will be humiliated?"

I rolled my eyes. "Here we go."

"They've been pretty supportive so far," she reminded me.

"That's because nobody outside the family knows yet. Wait till I become the gossip of the town and people start calling me a freak."

She leaned toward me. "Why do you care so much about what other people think?" "Um, because we live in a SOCIETY."

"Maybe you should stop caring so much about society so you can start focusing more on what you need to do to be happy."

"Easy for you to say." I turned away from Bet and gazed out the tiny window to the left of her head, wishing I could fit through it.

"Well, look where it's gotten you so far," she reasoned. "I'm just suggesting you step back and think about what's best for you—what will give you the best chances of success in transitioning so that you come out of this healthy and adjusted. You're going to have to undergo a "real-life test" where you live as a man for six months before you're eligible for any medical procedures, and after that you'll have to go through not one but likely a series of surgeries that could take years. It might be much harder and much more stressful for you to move to another state where you have no family or friends for support and try to do all that in secret."

She had me there. My family hadn't shunned me. And while they wanted me to reconsider, they had promised to stand by me, whatever I decided to do. My friends, well, I guess if they don't support me they were never really my friends to begin with. It would be easier not having to move. Packing would suck, especially all the glassware and kitchen stuff . . . *Wait, was I actually rethinking this? Crap.*

"Well, I guess if I stayed in Boston I could leave Arnold and find another job."

"Why would you need to leave Arnold?" Bet said.

"Are you kidding me?!" Now she was pushing it.

"You love your job. You love the people you work with. Why do you have to give that up?"

Ah, because I'm scared shitless and I literally and figuratively don't have the balls. "Because I couldn't do that to my dad."

"Having met your father, I believe he would want you to do whatever was easiest for you. If that meant staying at Arnold, I bet he'd support that."

"So you think staying at Arnold and becoming a man in front of the entire agency would be easier than just getting a job somewhere else as a man where no one knew me before?"

"I don't know," she said. "I'm just asking you to think about it. Sometimes it's easier to do something openly. Over time it's a lot less stressful when you're not worried about people finding out your big secret."

Me? *Not* worried? Did she forget that I'm a worrier by nature? That I stress over EVERYTHING. In high school I was voted "Most Likely to Get an Ulcer," for god's sake. So when it came to changing my gender in front of everyone I knew, I was *consumed* with worry—worry about what people were going to think or say or do. It was paralyzing.

But Bet helped me realize something that would become the single most important guiding principle both during and after my transition: *I had the ability to control the way people responded to me—that the way I acted could actually shape the way others reacted.* If I came off ashamed or secretive, people would gossip and rumors would spread. But if I handled myself openly with dignity and grace, people would treat me in kind. If I was approachable and lighthearted, they would feel comfortable around me. If I was patient, encouraged questions, and took the time to help them understand, they would have an open mind and come to accept me for who I was.

Something in my head clicked. It was like Bet had unlocked a secret inner power I didn't know I had—one that gave me the balls to take control of my transition and my life and do what I needed to do to be happy.

The first step: a heart-to-heart with my dad.

••

"Dad, how would you feel if I stayed at Arnold and went through my transition? I want you to be honest. I can totally look for another job. It's not a big deal."

The poor man was at the kitchen table peacefully enjoying his nightly cookies and milk when I lobbed this grenade at him. I held my breath.

He stared at me earnestly and put down his half-eaten Oreo. "Kris, I want you to do whatever's best for you. Don't worry about me. You have enough to worry about. If you want to stay at Arnold, I'll support you."

All at once I felt so much love for my dad and so much fear for myself. A little part of me hoped he would say, "Absolutely not—find another job!" and spare me from having to muster up the tremendous amount of courage it was going to take to get through this next phase.

Before I could even enter that phase, I had some homework to do: I needed to come up with my "hit list"—a list of people I felt I needed to drop the "boy bomb" on in person. Bet had asked me to bring this to our next session. It was time to let people outside my immediate family in on my secret, and she was going to strategize with me and help come up with a game plan. When I finished my assignment, I had eighty-seven names, the first four of which were *Mom, Dad, Wendy,* and *Jill.* Yes, I had already told them, but I wrote their names down anyway just so I could cross them off and feel like I'd made some progress.

"Wow, you know all these people?" Bet said, examining the piece of paper.

"Yeah, I have a lot of friends."

"Okay, who do you think you'd like to start with?"

I'd actually been doing a lot of thinking about this and had two people in mind.

Since my mom seemed to be struggling with the idea of losing a daughter, it was important to me that she have someone she could confide in other than my dad and my therapist (she'd met with Bet a few times). So the first person I was going to tell was her sister, Barbara. I was very close with Aunty Barbie growing up. She was a kindergarten teacher and had a warm and nurturing way about her. I knew she'd be a good listener and felt the odds were also in my favor that she'd understand or at least try to, and then be there for my mom. I called her at home in Connecticut and less than thirty-six hours after hanging up with me, she was pulling into my parents' driveway. My parents were in Florida, but Jill and Wendy were with me for moral support, and soon the four of us were sitting on the navy blue leather sectional in tears. Mine began even before I opened my mouth.

"I've been diagnosed with gender dysphoria," I told Aunty.

"I know," she said. "Your mom told me in confidence this summer.

She didn't want me to tell you but I couldn't sit here and pretend like I didn't know."

I looked at my sisters and we all shook our heads. Mom was not known for her secret-keeping skills, but I couldn't be mad at her for this one. She'd needed someone to talk to, which was why I was telling Aunty in the first place. It just would have been nice to know she'd already taken the initiative.

"I'm sorry to make you drive all the way here," I said.

"Honey, it's two hours, I wanted to talk to you in person and I'm glad you were ready to open up to me."

She held my hand and we both cried as I told her how painful my life has been living as a girl.

"I just can't do it anymore, Aunty. Surgery is my only hope if I ever want to be happy. I was going to move away where nobody knew me and then go through it, but after talking with my therapist, I decided to stay here where I would at least have support from family and hopefully my friends."

I then laid out my plan to transition while still working at Arnold.

She told me how brave I was, but I could see fear in her eyes. I knew she was scared for me.

"You'll find out who your real friends are," she said. "To a true friend it won't make a difference whether you're male or female on the outside. You'll still be you on the inside and that's all that matters. If they can't deal with it then they weren't really your friends to begin with."

I nodded in agreement, knowing what she said was the truth, but it really didn't make me feel any better. There was nothing anyone could say to reassure me completely. In my world, this had never been done before. There was no experience or "best practices" I could draw from. No crystal ball. We both reached at the same time for the tissue box Jill had been hoarding.

As Aunty stood up to go, I gave her a copy of the one article I'd found that I thought did a great job explaining gender dysphoria in layman's terms. She asked me if I wanted her to share all this with my cousins. I told her Adam and Dana were on my hit list, but that it would make it easier for me to talk to them about it knowing it wouldn't be coming out of the blue. We hugged and she was gone. After closing the door behind her, I went back into the family room and flopped down on the couch where Wendy and Jill were still sitting. They looked almost as emotionally drained as I felt.

"I think that went well," Wendy said encouragingly.

"Who's next, Shtine?" Jill asked.

••

The next person on the list was also named Barbara. "Babs" was Wendy's closest friend and confidante. A coworker at Arnold, she was someone I considered a good friend too. I wanted Wendy to have an outsider she could talk to and Babs was perfect. Not only was she trustworthy, she knew our whole family and could act as a gauge for how my news would go over at the agency.

Still, in my mind it was a lot easier for friends to walk away than relatives. I had no idea how Babs would react. All she knew was that I had something important to tell her and it was serious. She tried to get some intel out of my sister but Wendy wouldn't bite.

We met for dinner at the Sail Loft, an old-school shanty overlooking Boston Harbor, one of our favorite spots. Babs swore their fish-and-chips were the best in all of New England, and I loved the fact that at the bar, instead of bowls of peanuts, there were jars of Oreos. (Like father, like son.)

It was there at a table by the bar that I choked. Well, not literally. I don't even think I took a bite of my chicken fingers. I had rehearsed what I was going to say to imaginary Barbara over and over in my head; but with the real Barbara staring back at me with a concerned and expectant look on her face, I got totally flustered. I couldn't remember where to start. I was all over the map and crying so much that the waitress wouldn't come near our table. That extra tartar sauce and honey mustard we asked for? Yeah, that wasn't happening.

Babs was clearly caught off guard by my revelation and the emotional unraveling happening before her eyes and those of everyone around us. I could tell she wanted to hug me but felt forced to hold her composure for the sake of appearances. She asked a question every now and then, in an attempt to fully process what I was saying, and did a lot of nodding to show her support. When we finally got up to leave with our uneaten dinners boxed to go, I apologized for making her my "guinea pig," letting her know she was the first one outside my family I'd told and that I chose her so she could be there for Wendy.

"I'll be there for you too, Shtine," she said, putting her arm around me.

"Thanks Babs. Sorry for the scene."

"I'm sure you'll get better at it with practice," she said. "Next time, though, you might want to tell people in the privacy of your own home."

We both laughed.

Babs was right: I did get better with practice, especially when it came to reining in my emotions. Some of my friends made it very easy for me, like Beth and Mandy, my next victims.

I'd actually come close to telling them a few times since that Monday morning after I found out about Jess's boyfriend. One night after a few drinks Mandy almost got it out of me. I stopped myself from telling her, but must've given her a pretty big clue, because the next day there was an envelope from her on my desk. Inside was a pencil sketch of some type of flower. I wasn't sure what to make of it until I noticed Mandy's handwriting on the back of her drawing. She wrote that she thought she'd figured out what I was going through and if she was right, I had a tough road ahead of me and was the bravest person she knew. That last line gave me the feeling she might have guessed correctly, but I couldn't be sure.

We picked a pub near the state house—close to the office, but not so close that we would run into anyone from work. It was chilly but we were prepared for the walk. Especially Beth, who was wearing the maroon winter coat Mandy and I dubbed "Old Faithful" because she wore it every day from November through March. We grabbed a table and the two of them sat across from me. Staring. Waiting.

"Ah, I'm gonna need a drink for this so you're gonna have to wait a bit longer." They groaned, and as if on cue, the cocktail waitress showed up. I motioned for them to order (*ladies first*), then I ordered two vodka sodas. The waitress looked confused.

"I'm thirsty," I said.

I downed the first drink and as soon as my empty glass hit the table, Mandy pounced.

"Alright, spill it."

Beth was nodding at me with encouragement in her eyes, so I squeezed the lime into my second drink, took a deep breath, and told them how when I was five I told my grandmother I wasn't a girl.

"Yes!" they shouted. "We knew it!"

I sat there dumbfounded while the two of them high-fived each other, congratulating themselves on their powers of deduction. Apparently they'd been having Nancy Drew sleuthing sessions for the past few months, and whatever clue I gave Mandy in my drunken stupor had led them down the right path.

"At first we thought you were gay," Beth said, "but that night when you said stuff like you wouldn't wish it on your worst enemy, we knew it had to be more serious than that. We also wondered if you might have cancer. Thank God you're okay."

They were so relieved everything was finally out in the open so they could be there for me. And so was I. I really wished I'd told them sooner. They ordered another round while I discussed moving away and my therapist's suggestion that I stay in Boston and transition at Arnold. I assumed they'd be just as taken aback by that idea as I initially had been, and the frightened part of me hoped they'd try to talk me out of it.

"Why wouldn't you?" was their response. "Your family supports you, we support you, and so will everyone else. Everybody loves you, Kris. Why would you move away and deal with this all by yourself when you don't have to?"

It was like Bet was whispering in their ear. I half expected her to show up with their beers and a nice tall glass of "I told you so" for me, which I would've chugged down gladly. I had just received the confirmation I needed, and at that moment I made my decision: I was going to become a man in Boston, at Arnold. But not before I made it through my hit list, which, thanks to Bet's guidance and a lot of practice, was getting shorter and shorter.

••

"I told Mary and Sheila."

"What'd they say?" my parents asked eagerly in unison.

Every Sunday I'd come home for dinner and list all the people I told that week, continually stunning my mom and dad with firsthand accounts of overwhelming acceptance and support.

"Why are you so surprised?" Jill said to them. "Everyone loves Shtiny."

Jill appeared to be right. So far I had told over twenty of my "targets," and while there were lots of blank faces, a few wide eyes, and one or two actual jaw drops, I had yet to receive any negative reactions. The key was scheduling the meetings a few days in advance and letting people know up front I had something serious to tell them. It gave them time to think about what it could possibly be and put them in the right frame of mind to hear this type of news. With each sit-down, I honed my technique, learning what worked and what didn't so I could better set myself up for success. Each time was a little bit easier than the last. One-on-ones, group sessions, it didn't matter where. I told my coworkers Mary and Sheila in my office with the door closed. I told my college friends and former rugby teammates in various locations: Hazel at her house, Diana in a booth at Friendly's, Quigley at a Mexican restaurant, and Price and Fedin together at my North End apartment. I dropped the bomb on three of my closest high school friends over drinks at an outdoor bar in Faneuil Hall.

Before I met with people, I had categorized them with a number from 1 to 3 (I'm not Type A; I'm Type A+). The number 1 meant "very likely to accept the news well," and 3 was "not sure what they'll do." I was building up my confidence, knocking off the 1s first, then the 2s, and leaving the 3s for last. But while I was making major progress, I was also realizing that telling eighty-seven people personally was not only ambitious but also unrealistic (not to mention expensive when I was picking up the tab every time).

So I started highlighting names that could be "second gens," which meant it would be okay for them to hear the news from someone else I had told personally. This made what and how I told people even more important. If I wanted them to deliver my news to others in a knowledgeable, accurate, and sensitive manner, then I had to deliver it to them the same way. I encouraged friends and coworkers to ask questions, knowing I was probably the first person they'd ever met who was transgender and that the questions they had were likely the same questions others would have. I didn't take it as an invasion of privacy, but rather an opportunity to educate and arm people with specific information I wanted them to know and share. I was open, honest, and ready with a joke to help make people more comfortable. When I asked a friend or coworker to tell someone else, I offered up my coaching services and had them practice on me—which was a very good idea!

All my efforts were paying off. For the first time in years I dared to envision a future for myself. There were no more thoughts of suicide. Some days I even woke up happy! And what made me even happier, the more positive outcomes I relayed to my parents, the more I noticed a shift in their attitudes about my decision to undergo gender reassignment. Their biggest fear was that I'd lose all my friends, become a social outcast, and end up worse off than I already was. With exactly the opposite happening, they were feeling much better about the idea of me transitioning. Instead of simply accepting my decision, they began to embrace it. Especially my mom who, bolstered by courage, confidence, and a cordless phone, went on a full-blown "telling spree." In one week after turning herself loose, she had told almost our entire extended family and by the week after that, Dad's and her close friends. She'd call me every now and then asking for tips, like "Shtine, how did you start?" or "What term should I use instead of *sex change*?"

On one of those calls I reminded her to refer to the article on gender dysphoria I'd given her.

"Oh right," she said. "Can you make me another copy of it? I sent mine to Gram."

"Gram knows?!"

I was picturing my seventy-six-year-old grandmother in her pink St. John knit pantsuit with the black trim, jaw resting on the bows of her black patent leather Ferragamos.

"Yes, I told her in Florida. She's writing you a letter."

I thought back to the conversation Gram and I had when I was five and wondered if she remembered it. Since then we'd remained extremely close. She showed me how to swing a golf club, keep score at bowling, and play backgammon and card games like canasta and her favorite, Head & Foot. She babysat my sisters and me right up through high school, taught me how to drive, and even got me drunk for the first time. Granted I was twelve and it was from eating too much of her Peach Melba, but I passed out, so it still counts. She was on my hit list for sure, but I wasn't ready to tell her yet (she was a 3). I just didn't think someone from her generation would understand. Part of me was relieved Mom took care of it for me, but the bigger part of me was worried how Gram would treat me now that she knew.

"Well?" I asked my mom. "What did she say when you told her?"

"That it all made sense."

Gram's letter arrived the following week. It was handwritten on off-white unlined paper—two pages front and back—and began, "My Darling Kris." She wrote how sad she felt that I had been suffering inside all these years. She remembered that day I told her I was a boy and said that it all made sense to her now; the way I dressed, the toys I wanted for Christmas. I had always been "boyish" and she suspected I might be a "mannish lesbian." She went on to express her worries about whether or not I would be able to pass as a man. She never actually used the term "pass" but described her concern by telling me about a hairdresser that worked at the beauty shop she went to. She said this woman was a lesbian who "dressed like a man in pants and blazers" but her body and features still made her look like a woman. She wondered if the hormones or even surgery would be able to make my body look masculine enough for people to see me as a man. "Will you still have smooth skin and a round butt like females do? This is what worries me, darling," she wrote. "Will you be happy with the way you look? Will people accept you?" She ended by telling me that more than anything she wanted me to be happy.

She signed it "All my love, Gram."

Gram's fears were not unfounded. Mainstream society has a very binary view when it comes to how a man or woman should look. If people who are transgender can't conform to that narrow view and "pass" as the gender they affirm, they are much more likely to experience discrimination and violence. This is where privilege plays a big role; having access to quality medical care and the money to pay for surgeries that help feminize or masculinize appearance is a big advantage. One I was very lucky to have.

I stayed up late writing back to her, belaboring every word. I answered her concerns with assurances that I would be able to pass as a man, adding that just the other day a carful of girls honked and whistled at me while I was crossing the street. (I had on a baseball cap and bulky jacket.) I told her that the hormones would alter my facial features and redistribute my body fat and that surgery would hopefully take care of the rest, but that no matter how I looked I would be happier than I am now, because it couldn't get any worse. I wrote how accepting my friends had been so far and how truly lucky I felt to have such a loving and supportive family. I ended by telling her how much I loved her and that I hoped the closeness of our relationship wouldn't change, even if I did.

When Gram came home from Florida at the end of April, I was nervous to see her. But when I walked into my parents' kitchen for Sunday dinner there she was, the same smile and outstretched arms embracing me with the same love as before.

Gram's acceptance gave me the courage to knock another "3" off my list—my roommate, Jim. Because of our history, I wasn't sure how he would take the news. Would he be disgusted at having had romantic feelings for me? Would he be embarrassed when word got out to mutual friends who'd known how he'd felt about me years ago? He was recently engaged and planning to move in with his fiancée in a few months anyway. I figured if he was repulsed by me, he could always move out sooner. So I told him I had something important I needed to talk to him about, and we set up a night to both be home at the apartment. Jim sat there on the couch waiting patiently for me to come out with it, and after I did, he couldn't understand why I was so afraid to tell him.

"What did you think I was going to say?" he asked gently.

"I wasn't sure. You used to have feelings for me and I didn't know how this would affect you . . . I was nervous you wouldn't want to be friends anymore."

Jim gave me a hug. "You're still the same person."

That might be, but as I'd later discover, it didn't get me an invitation to his wedding.

"I'm really sorry," he confessed during a game of eight-ball. "I wanted to invite you, but then I was thinking how you knew my whole family and most of my friends and they knew how I'd felt about you and I . . . I just chickened out."

That stung.

"Jim, I totally understand, but I gotta tell you that hurts. We've been close friends for five years, roommates for two. I never expected I wouldn't get an invitation."

He looked down at the pool table.

"Just so you know, had I gotten one, my plan was to gracefully decline for all the reasons you just said. I would never want to make you feel uncomfortable at your own wedding—I would've been uncomfortable too. I appreciate your honesty. I just wish it had come sooner so we could've talked it through together."

"You're right," he said, "I'm really sorry."

I could tell Jim felt horrible about it and I couldn't hold it against him; he was a good guy. There was no protocol for a situation like this. I could've brought it up first and told him not to invite me. It wasn't fair to put it all on him. So I accepted his apology and made my forgiveness contingent on him buying the next round of beers.

We left on great terms that night, but we never really hung out again. I sometimes wonder if we'd still be friends had I not changed my gender.

Maybe we would've naturally grown apart; he was getting married, moving to the suburbs, and starting a family. Still, when people ask me if I lost any friends because of my transition, my response is "Yes, just one."

OPERATION: EVANGELISTS

May 1995

"Wow, Kris, you're really making progress," Bet said, looking over my hit list, now half-covered in cross-outs and color-coded highlighting. "Who are the people you have left here?"

"Ah, those are mostly people I work with. Coworkers, bosses."

"Hmmm . . ."

Oh no, here it comes.

"I think it's time we start talking about your plan for coming out at the agency."

I knew it.

"So," I asked, "have you ever had a patient transition like this, you know, publicly at a large company?" (With the Volkswagen win, Arnold's Boston office was now up to five hundred employees.)

"No."

Great.

"But, with the right strategy," she added, "you'll get through this successfully. You've already demonstrated you can handle it."

"Uh-huh. So how does one go about this process? Who do I tell first to make it official? The head of HR?"

"You could. That's probably what some people do. But you're in a unique position. Your father is the head of the company. Let's use that to your advantage."

Okay, now I was confused. When it came to going public, I never saw that as an advantage—more as a humiliation for my dad and an additional reason for people to talk. I wasn't just some random female employee about to become a man. I was the owner/CEO's daughter. Advantage? That's a good one.

"How can this be an advantage?"

"Well," Bet said, "there must be an executive board, right?"

I nodded slowly, not liking where this was going.

"And your father could get you into one of those meetings."

Yup, this woman has lost her mind.

"You want me to make an announcement to the executive board?!" I laughed, shaking my head in disbelief. *Hello, twelve conservative men I've said no more than two words to in the hallway. Let me share my most intimate feelings with you and tell you all about my how my body parts don't match my gender . . .*

"Just hear me out here. You know people are going to talk, and it will reflect better on you *and* your dad if the board hears about this directly from you and not the gossip mill. Better it come from the top and trickle down."

Again, I shook my head. This ordeal was going to be hard enough without the added stress of a boardroom coming-out party. That being said, she did have a point. *Shit.*

"Okay, so I tell the board. And assuming none of them croaks at the conference table, then what? They call an agency meeting?"

"Well, maybe they send out a memo."

"A MEMO? I don't think so."

"Well, you could tell them what you'd like them to do. How would you have them handle it?"

As I mulled this over on my way back to work, it hit me: I wouldn't have *them* handle it at all.

At the time, the latest trend in advertising was evangelism marketing (today it's called word-of-mouth marketing, or WOMM). The idea at its core is basically getting people who love your brand to actively recommend it to others. Our goal at Arnold was to turn consumers into brand evangelists for our clients. So I figured, why not turn my coworkers into brand evangelists for me? I had already done this on a targeted scale when I enlisted friends to tell the "second gens" on my hit list. So I knew it could work. I would tell a core group of coworkers my story personally, coach them on how to pass it on, and then immediately after the executive board meeting, give them the green light to start spreading the word throughout the agency.

I ran my idea by Beth and Mandy. They thought it was brilliant and were honored to be my first two evangelists. They gave me feedback on what had struck a chord with them and what they found confusing to better help me fine-tune my story. I jotted down some notes and made a list of ten more coworkers I considered part of my Arnold inner circle (some of whom, like Mary and Sheila, were on my hit list and had been told already). With my strategy now mapped out, I decided to pay Dad a visit at home for an impromptu Wednesday-night dinner. This couldn't wait until Sunday.

He stared at me with sympathy—sympathy mixed with the pride a father feels when his child is about to undertake something dauntingly noble.

"You want to tell the executive board?"

He sounded somewhat pained. I told him my plan, adding that it had been endorsed by Bet to give it some psychiatric cred. He listened intently and then nodded his agreement. "I'll tell them."

"What?"

"I'll tell the board. You have enough on your plate already."

"Are you sure, Dad?

"Yes. Let me do this for you."

I could tell he really needed to. It was an opportunity for him to take some of the weight off my shoulders—something any parent would want to do for their child—and frankly, I was happy to have the out. It was a win-win.

The board met once a month, and Dad promised to let me know the next meeting date as soon as possible so I could back out a timetable for "Operation: Evangelists." My plan was to begin having one-on-ones a week or two beforehand to minimize the leakage factor—it's always easier to keep a secret the sooner you're allowed to tell it.

Well, for most people . . . My dad, it turns out, was the exception. He wanted to be my biggest evangelist, but he hadn't found his voice yet.

••

"We told the Pratts and the Orrs," Mom announced triumphantly over the phone.

"Did you tell them or did Dad?"

"I told them, of course. Your father hasn't told anybody yet."

I couldn't get those last six words out of my head. I had been feeling more and more uncomfortable about Dad taking on the responsibility of telling the board and I'd finally realized why: He hadn't had any practice telling anyone. There was no way he was ready for something this big. I could coach him, but the fact remained: I was the one who could tell my story best, and the more I thought about it, the more strongly I felt that the news should come directly from me. There was way too much riding on this meeting, now just three weeks away. I had to say something.

I arrived early for Sunday dinner to find my mom in the kitchen negotiating a stack of pots and pans.

"Hi, Shtine, can you put this pan up top for me?" (You know my mom's short when she has to ask someone who's barely 5'4" for help.)

"Sure, Mom. Where's Dad?"

"He's in the bedroom going through his closet. He's threatening to buy some new shorts. All the ones he has make him look like he's wearing diapers."

I laughed. "Hey, so Mom, I've been thinking it might be better if I was the one to tell the executive board, not Dad. But I know he really wanted to do it. Do you think he'd be hurt if I—"

"Oh, he'd be re-lieeeeved. He's been stressing over it for the last two weeks. He's never really had to tell anyone, you know. I always do it."

"Yes, I know. And you do a great job!" I kissed her on the cheek and ventured to the master bedroom where Dad was standing in front of his side of the walk-in closet (the smaller side), his feet surrounded by five or six pairs of shorts in varying degrees of khaki.

"Get rid of them all," I said, deadpan.

"You're here early. Hey, you need any Bermuda shorts? I got a bunch of these I'm getting rid of." (This would become a ritual between us; Dad trying to pawn his clothes off on me despite our obvious size difference.)

"No thanks, Dad. Gauchos are out of style. Hey listen, I've been thinking about the board meeting. I really appreciate you wanting to be the one to tell them, but I think it should probably come from me. It will show I respect them and that I'm not ashamed. Plus I've been telling the story over and over now for months so I might be able to explain it better and answer any questions they have directly. What do you think?"

Mom was right. While he tried not to show it, he was clearly relieved. "Yes, sure, if that's what you want. I mean I'm happy to do it, but you're probably right . . . I could set you up?"

"Yes! Great idea. It'll set the tone and show you support what I'm doing."

"Okay, that's what we'll do."

He smiled warmly, then turned his eyes back toward the closet. "Hey how 'bout some golf shirts . . . Look, look at this one—never been worn."

"I gave you that one."

"That's why I thought you'd like it."

●●

With just one week to go until the board meeting, my dad's assistant, Marilyn, called to let me know "Big Ed" wanted to see me in his office. A proud mom in her mid-forties, she had a great sense of humor and a penchant for brightly colored pens and paper clips. Her good nature and calming presence made her an office favorite. She'd only been with my dad a few years, but already felt like part of our family.

When I arrived she was fielding a call. *Did Marilyn know? She had to. Mom surely must have told her.* They talked on the phone pretty much every day, and Mom was on a telling spree . . . I gave her a wave and headed straight into Dad's well-appointed corner office, the inside of which remained a mystery to most of the agency. I crossed the Oriental rug, passed the wall of framed advertising-themed *New Yorker* cartoons, and made myself as comfortable as possible in one of the stiff wingback leather guest chairs across from his ginormous yet elegant desk. No longer on the creative floor, I looked incredibly out of place in my faded Levi's, untucked Polo, and Jack Purcell sneakers.

"You goin' to wash your car?" Dad asked.

"Ha ha. What's up?"

"Well, I hate to do this to you, but I had to move the board meeting."

My stomach dropped.

"I have to go to Germany for a big VW meeting. I didn't think I'd have to but the client wants me there."

Fuck! "That's okay," I said, trying to mask my disappointment. "I understand."

"I've asked Marilyn to reschedule it for the following week. She'll let you know as soon as she nails down the day."

"Okay. Hey, Marilyn knows, right?"

"Yeah. She saw that article you gave us on my desk, so I told her."

"You did?" I said, impressed.

"Well . . . I started to," he admitted, "but she said she already knew. Your mother told her."

On my way out I stopped at Marilyn's desk. "So the meeting is being rescheduled," I griped.

"Yep."

I sighed.

"You know, Kris, I think you're very brave."

"Thanks, Marilyna." (I always called her that.)

"Can I give you some advice?"

"Sure."

"If you're gonna get a penis, make it a big one."

••

T minus three days and four hours: I am a nervous wreck, unable to think about anything else. I keep rehearsing what I'm going to say to the board in my head, trying to identify potential red flags, and imagining all kinds of hypothetical outcomes. It's all I can think of that Sunday as I drive to my parents' house on autopilot and pull into the empty space in the driveway between my sisters' cars.

"Happy Father's Day!" I announce, entering the house, gift in hand.

Dad was sitting in his chair watching golf, TV remote securely in his grasp. Mom and Gram were in the kitchen. Wendy and Jill were nowhere to be seen, which meant they were up in their old bedrooms surveying the contents of their closets and making sure every item was still present and accounted for.

"Hey, Shtiny," Dad yelled. I put the gift on the counter with the others, next to mom's homemade chocolate layer cake with the "hard" chocolate frosting (Dad's favorite), kissed Mom and Gram, and headed over to give Dad a hug.

"Want a cuke?" he asked, passing me a small plate of crudités akin to the larger one sitting on the coffee table untouched.

I took a cucumber slice and mid-crunch he broke the news.

"I had to move the board meeting again."

Noooooooooooo!

"I meant to tell you on Friday . . . four out of the eight members couldn't make it so it's now gonna be next Monday."

Great. I had a pit in my stomach the size of a cannonball and now it would be lodged there for another eight freaking days.

That week at work I was in a fog. I could barely concentrate, let alone come up with any award-winning headlines. Instead I spent most of the time discussing the anxiety I felt about Monday's upcoming event with my team of evangelists, who looked at me with sympathy each time I showed up in their respective offices with word of another postponement. No one had leaked the news (as far as I knew), which confirmed that I had entrusted my secret to the right people.

By Thursday afternoon I felt like a prisoner counting down to his parole hearing when, as if on cue, the phone at my desk rang. I recognized my dad's extension.

"Hey, Kris. Um, I'm sorry to do this to you again but we need to move the meeting."

"What?! Are you serious?" I could feel myself crumbling inside.

"Yeah, Ron can't make it now, so I thought we should change it since he's probably the most important one from your standpoint."

"No, Dad, I can't go through this again. It has to be Monday. I'll tell Ron myself beforehand. Just please, please DO NOT cancel it." My voice was elevated and quivering. I was ready to lose it. I managed to hold it together, though mostly because there was a nosy art director hovering outside my office.

Dad's voice became softer and more sympathetic. "Okay, we'll leave it on Monday. Ron's going out of town though, so you should try to get to him soon."

I hung up and immediately called Ron's assistant. She told me he was off Friday and was flying out of town Monday afternoon. *Shit!*

"Do you need to show him concepts?" she asked.

"No."

"Present radio? He's done that over the phone a few times."

"No, it's not really work-related."

"Oh . . ." I could tell she was curious and was bracing myself for more questions. "Well, if it's important I could squeeze you in Monday during his lunch hour. Just be at your desk between twelve and one and I'll call you when he's ready."

Phew. I hung up, took a deep breath, and looked up at the clock. 4:15.

Fuck it. I'm going home.

••

Sunday, T minus twenty-seven hours. Instead of the kitchen, we're all in my parents' dining room. The mood around the table is somber. I'm getting the sense that my family is likening this afternoon's meal to the Last Supper. I, on the other hand, feel oddly upbeat. Dare I say, even a little bit excited. Maybe it's because I've had so much practice telling people that I'm feeling confident and well rehearsed. Maybe it's because this meeting has been hanging over my head for a month and a half and I'm finally going to get it over with. Whatever the reason, I assure my family, mainly for the benefit of my dad, that I am up to the task and looking forward to getting past this monumental step. Nobody says it, but we all know that after my announcement at tomorrow's board meeting, none of our lives will ever be the same.

After dinner, Dad asked me if I wanted to take a ride to Ogilvie's, the local hardware store. I loved going there with him as a kid, because in addition to all the cool tools and stuff, they had a lollipop tree at the register with Dum Dums, free for the taking. Knowing Dad's propensity for luring us into the car with a quick errand we might enjoy and then holding us hostage while he completed the rest of his secret to-do list, I made sure I used the bathroom before we left. For all I knew, he had dry cleaning hidden in the trunk, a gas tank on empty, bills that had to be mailed, and an urgent need to get the car washed before it rained. I also suspected he wanted to talk to me about the meeting tomorrow. My suspicion was confirmed when, after leaving Ogilvie's, he turned left onto Route 20 instead of right.

"Hey," he said, "there's a house I wanna show you over on Meadow-brook." Read: *I need to extend the duration of the ride so I can talk to you about something.*

"Okay . . ." There was silence for a few seconds and then he began. "So I was thinking about tomorrow and what I was gonna say . . . I had Marilyn put your name as the last item on the agenda so it wouldn't be a surprise when you came in."

"Oh, good idea."

"I figured the meeting starts at four o'clock, so you should come down around five and wait outside the board room. I'll have them break for a few minutes and then come out and get you."

"Good plan." *Wow, he's really thought this through.*

"I was gonna introduce you . . . I mean set you up—you'll know everyone there."

As he rattled off the members' names, I pictured them all in my head. Seven wealthy, middle-aged men, all white, all likely Republican, and all with backgrounds in account service or finance—the conservative departments in the agency. *Oh boy.*

"Ron won't be there," Dad reminded me. "Did you talk to him already?"

"No, he was out Friday. I'm going to tell him tomorrow around noon. Before he leaves for the airport."

"Oh . . ."

I read Dad's hesitation as worry—worry that would be too much for me in one day.

"It'll be like a warm-up for the main event," I joked.

He laughed and then took me through what he had planned to say in his setup. It went something like this:

> You've all probably noticed Kris' name on the agenda. Kris has been dealing with something serious for a long time and up until now has confided only in family and close friends who've all been very understanding and supportive, including myself. The next year or so is going to be very challenging and Kris is going to need our support as an agency to help get through it. We both felt it would be best for you to hear it directly from Kris.

I told Dad it was a perfect setup and that I wouldn't change a thing. I especially loved how he didn't use pronouns. That night I slept well, knowing that tomorrow he would be in my corner.

●●

Ironically, the day I spent the most time in the ladies' room at Arnold was also the same day I announced to the board I was really a man. It was 4:45 p.m., and I had peed around twenty-six times. The only thing I got done that day was a lot of flushing. This is what I'm thinking about as I take the stairwell down to the tenth floor on my way to the boardroom. It occurs to me that today it should be called the "board-doom," and I congratulate myself for such stellar word play. *Good one, Shtine!* It was comforting to know that even in the face of the most nerve wracking event of my life, I could still keep my sense of humor. Even if only for a moment.

As I approached Marilyn's desk we locked eyes, mine filled with dread, hers with sympathy. "They're still in there," she said.

"I'm a little early."

"You're just like your father," she said, and then perfectly imitated him as only an assistant can. *"If you're not early, you're late."*

I smiled. "So I hear I'm actually on the agenda."

"Yep, typed it up myself."

She handed me her copy to look at. There I was, right next to *5:00 p.m.* and just after the words *coffee break.*

"Your dad figured it would be a good excuse to break, and give people something to do while he left the room to come out and get you."

Again, I'd underestimated my father. That was pretty smart. It'd be easier for me to walk in there if people were up and around chatting and not sitting in their seats gazing at me expectantly, although that would happen eventually, I was sure.

"You ready?"

"As I'll ever be. I told Ron earlier today. At lunch."

"Ooh. How'd that go?"

"It was awkward. He had a plane to catch so I only had fifteen minutes. The poor guy hadn't even taken two bites of his sandwich when I lowered the boom. I don't think he knew what to say, so I just kept talking so he wouldn't have to say anything. But in classic Ron fashion he boiled it down to one line: *'That must've been really hard.'* I told him I was announcing it to the board, and since he couldn't be at the meeting I wanted him to know first. I think he appreciated that. Anyway, it was good practice, right?"

"You're gonna do great," Marilyn said and then picked up her ringing phone. As she told whoever it was that Mr. Eskandarian was not available, I looked up at the clock. Five on the nose. And I had to pee again. *What if I go and I'm not here when they're ready for me? I'll just hold it. No, then I'll be distracted. I'll go really fast.* I got Marilyn's attention while she was on the phone and pointed to the restrooms. She nodded and signaled for me to go quick.

When I returned, the door to the boardroom was still closed. Phew. I sat down in Marilyn's guest chair and took a deep breath. I looked down at my hands, which were shaking slightly on my lap, and noticed a small blue ballpoint pen mark on the thigh of my pants. I wasn't sure what to wear to this shindig, so I left the jeans at home and went for gender-neutral corporate casual: Gap flat-front khakis and a light blue linen shirt. Just as I began to wonder if my wardrobe selection too closely resembled that of "Pat" from *Saturday Night Live*, the door to the boardroom opened and my dad came out.

Showtime.

●●

The "board-doom" was roughly the size of two large offices. In the center of the room was a long dark mahogany table, which throughout my high school years sat in our dining room. But even if my mom strolled in with a tray of desserts to go with the coffee everyone was drinking, there was no way I was going to feel the slightest bit at home sitting at this table. Well, unless she served her famous Heath Bar Pie, then maybe . . . no, not even then.

With the exception of one of the men who was sporting the traditional navy blazer with gold buttons, all seven board members were rocking full-on suits and ties. I sat down next to my father at the head of the table, feeling underdressed but thankful I wasn't wearing jeans, and waited anxiously for everyone to finish fixing their coffee and return to their seats. Knowing Dad had an eloquent setup prepared was the only thing that helped calm my nerves. With the group now seated, I tried to control my breathing and waited for my father to speak. He cleared his throat and began.

"I'm sure you've all noticed Kris's name on the agenda. Kris has something very important to share with you. So, Kris . . . "

Wait, what?

With all eyes on me, I turned to Dad to see if that was really it. He looked back at me apologetically, then stared down at the table.

Yup.

I squeezed his arm to let him know it was okay, took a deep breath, and turned to the group, using humor as my segue. "Thank you, Dad, for that lengthy introduction."

Then I was in the zone. I spoke about how I'd been going through something extremely difficult. That as far back as I could remember I'd always known I was different. Felt different. I recounted the conversation I'd had with my grandmother when I was five, and that's when I noticed expressions start to change; pieces were being put together. Some of the men could no longer make eye contact with me and seemed to find their half-filled china coffee cups suddenly very interesting. The rest just appeared uncomfortable, probably wondering why I was sharing such personal details with them in the first place. But I kept going, knowing that Beth, Mandy, and a pitcher of margaritas were waiting for me. When I got to the part about wanting to kill myself after graduation, one of the men looked from me to my father with such heartbreak that I thought I saw his eyes well up, but I couldn't be sure because his glasses were so thick.

I explained I'd been diagnosed with gender dysphoria, which meant I had the thoughts, feelings, and emotions of a man but the body of a woman and gave them my patented looking-in-the-mirror anecdote. I told them there's no definitive answer as to why this happens to people—that many doctors believe, as do I, that it's biological and has to do with exposure to hormone levels in the womb that in turn affect brain chemistry. That diagnoses are conservatively estimated to be one in fifty thousand, but there's no way to really know for sure.[3] Finally, I told them that for many people, changing their gender via surgery is the only course of action that will bring happiness, and with the support of my family and friends that was the option I would be pursuing.

I paused to let that sink in. After an awkward silence, I invited them to ask questions: "I understand that I'm probably the only person you've ever met who is going through this, let alone talking about it publicly, so I'm very open to answering any questions. And if you share my story with anyone else, please reiterate that offer as well. I'd rather people get accurate information from me directly than gossip and spread misinformation."

After an even longer awkward silence, Blue Blazer spoke up. "I have a question, Kris: What can we do to help make this process easier for you?"

Wow. That was way more than I thought I was going to get. I smiled and allowed myself to breathe for the first time after my fifteen-minute monologue.

Dad chimed in to help steer the conversation, "Kris, why don't you tell them a bit about the next stage in the process and what steps you're planning to take."

"Okay, sure. Well, surgery happens over a few years and not right away. The first thing I'll be doing is what they call 'transitioning,' which means essentially living full-time as a man. I'll still go by 'Kris,' but I'll be spelling it with a C-h instead of a K, and asking people to use male pronouns. I'll be starting to dress and look more decidedly masculine, begin taking hormones, and you know, using the men's room."

And that's when, as the expression goes, *shit got real.*

Gasping, murmuring, eyes darting all around.

I couldn't believe it. After everything I'd said, my using the men's room was the thing that freaked them all out? There were eight men's rooms at the agency, one on every floor. Chances of any of these men bumping into me were slim to none since none of them worked on fourteen, which is where I'd be going most of the time.

---

3   For transgender estimates, see: https://ow.ly/10DKkz.

"We should send out a memo," someone suggested.

And with that, my dad officially snapped.

"WE'RE NOT SENDING OUT A MEMO!"

I put my hand on his arm and calmly addressed the group. "You won't need to send out a memo. I have twelve of my closest Arnold friends waiting in the wings. They know once this meeting ends to begin spreading the word. Trust me, come this time tomorrow, the entire advertising community will know. Also, I don't plan to use the men's rooms or the ladies' rooms at the agency for the next two weeks, just to give everyone enough time to let this sink in. I'll be using the unisex bathroom around the corner at Rebecca's Cafe. Believe me, I've thought this through."

Before anyone could say anything else, Dad stood up and announced that I would be leaving now and walked me to the door. I wasn't expecting him to follow me out, but he did; and as soon as he closed the door behind us, I lost my composure and completely broke down. My father hugged me and told me how proud he was of me. I was so physically and emotionally drained, his embrace was the only thing holding me up. Marilyn joined in to form a hug teepee, and now all three of us were crying. As we parted ways, Dad asked me to call him later but I told him I would most likely be drunk, so I would talk to him tomorrow.

The margaritas couldn't come fast enough. Neither could the elevator. I was anxious to get the hell out of the building without seeing anybody and pressed the down button at least twenty times before it finally showed up, thankfully with no one else inside. I knew I was safe once those doors closed, because from my dad's floor it was express to the lobby. What I didn't know was that while I made my escape to Mandy's apartment, Dad was back in front of the board laying out his expectations that they be supportive, be respectful, and not discuss this with the press under any circumstances. The press still found out—this was big news—and a few reporters did contact my dad directly. But they respected his request to keep it out of the papers and trade pubs. Mainly because they respected him and the way he treated them.

Respect. That's what made a difference for my father in that room and throughout his career. And it's what made a difference for me before, during, and after my transition. I respected how it would feel to *hear* the news, not just tell it. It all comes back to what Bet taught me: that the way I acted would dictate how other people reacted. I now knew intuitively that making others feel comfortable and having the patience to help them understand was the best way for me to get through this transition successfully—even if that meant for the next two weeks I'd have to take an elevator down fourteen floors and walk a quarter mile to pee.

THE MORNING AFTER

June 28, 1995

When I woke up the next morning, the only bad taste in my mouth was from the tequila. I was proud of the way I'd handled things and had I been given a do-over, I wouldn't have changed a thing. Still, I was dreading going into work and facing everyone. I considered staying home, but knew if I did that, people would think I was ashamed. Nope. I was walking into the agency with my head held high . . . at 8:30 in the morning when no one on my floor would be in yet.

I sat at my desk, staring at the computer but seeing nothing. A little after nine, I began to hear signs of life out in the halls. Here we go.

At 9:25 my first visitor arrived: a flamboyantly gay PR director in his late thirties and a sexual harassment suit waiting to happen. His favorite pastimes were making straight guys squirm and straight girls question what they wore to work that day. Of all people. I wasn't ready for his brand of sarcasm but braced myself for it as he entered my office. And then I noticed the tears in his eyes. "Stand up and give me a hug," he demanded in his usual bossy tone. "You are so brave. I'm so proud of you."

No jokes, no insults. I was stunned.

A few minutes later the art director I partnered with popped his head in my doorway. He was one of the people I confided in and was always quick with a joke to keep things light. Today was no exception.

"Morning, Kris . . . or should I say *Chris*."

"Good one, Martin. How long you been sittin' on that gem?"

"I thought of it on the train this morning. How'd it go yesterday?"

Before I could answer him, the head of print production showed up looking rushed, frazzled, and all business, per usual.

"I just talked to Mary and Sheila," she said cheerfully. "When you're ready, let me know how you want your name on your new business cards."

Wow.

It was like this all day. Account directors on pieces of business I worked on came by to offer their support and discuss how I wanted to handle informing clients. Coworkers swung by to let me know, in their own way, they were cool with my decision, in awe of my guts, or to just wish me the best. I got lots of hugs and a few handwritten notes. One of my buddies in the art studio gave me a bar mitzvah card. It said, "Congratulations, today you are a man" and on the inside he customized it to include guy tips—like always look straight ahead at the urinal. *What is it with the bathroom?*

Now I don't mean to imply that everybody who heard the news made a point to acknowledge it with me. Most people simply continued to treat me as they had before. Which was really all I wanted.

Word spread through the agency in all sorts of ways. The head of broadcast called her whole department together to put a stop to any gossip before it started. She set the tone by saying I'd come to a life-changing decision and that everyone in my family was behind me including my father, adding, "Ron and I are also behind Chris, so nobody better fuck with him." When she asked if there were any questions, the first one out of the gate was, "Are we all going to be on *Oprah,* and if so, what should we wear?"

Of course, there were reactions that were not exactly positive—mostly from people who didn't work with me directly or know me that well. But there were really only a handful of incidents I knew about and thankfully none were to my face. An account director known for his excessive brownnosing stopped by my dad's office to say he was "sorry to hear the news" about me and felt "even sorrier" for my dad. Dad told him there was nothing to be sorry about and asked him to leave. One of the group heads on a major account I didn't even work on called an "emergency" team meeting to discuss the "situation." Luckily, one of my evangelists was also a leader on the account and set him straight in front of everyone in the room.

My marketing strategy was working; my "brand" was being promoted and defended from all sides.

But not everyone could be converted. One of my most passionate evangelists told a group of female creatives who were gossiping about me how difficult my life had been and how brave she thought I was for doing this. One of the women brushed it off with, "Well, it's a lot easier when your father owns the company."

Really? *You* try it.

In light of all I'd been through and what was still to come, the comment really bothered me. Honestly, though, if that was the worst of it, that was pretty damned good. I'm sure there was more talk I didn't know about, but what I didn't know couldn't hurt me, so I refused to think about it. I made it through my first day at Arnold as Chris and walked out with my head held higher than when I walked in—and this time made sure it was at a time when there were plenty of people around to see me do it.

Was I fortunate to work at a progressive ad agency in liberal Boston, capital of one of the bluest blue states, and not for a more conservative corporation like, say, Procter & Gamble in Ohio? Absolutely. And did it help that my father was the CEO? You bet your ass. As much as that creative's dismissive response bothered me, she did have a point: Ninety percent of transgender employees are harassed, mistreated, or discriminated against at work, and more than a quarter said they were fired because of their transition.[4] Having job protection definitely helped, but did not make it "easy." My coworkers had the same negative frame of reference my family and friends had with those shocking movie and

---

4   Source for work statistics: https://www.americanprogress.org/issues/lgbt/news/2011/06/02/9872/
gay-and-transgender-people-face-high-rates-of-workplace-discrimination-and-harassment.

talk-show depictions of transgender people. I still had to change perceptions, and as anyone who works in advertising will tell you, that is the
furthest thing from easy.

My strategy was to be myself through it all. Show everyone that while
my gender might be changing, the essence of me wasn't: I was still "Me,"
just "Me 2.0." And one thing everyone loved about me was my sense of
humor. Remembering Bet's advice about how I had the power to control
the way people reacted, I took every opportunity where appropriate to
make light of my situation and put people at ease. It was my way of letting
them know my transition was a topic open for discussion, and that they
didn't have to avoid me for fear of saying the wrong thing.

The first time I joked about my gender change was like an involun-
tary reaction. I was walking down the hall past the agency's editing suite
just as the head of AV held up an adapter cord and said to her intern,
"This is a female to male." The timing was too perfect. I popped my
head inside the doorway and said, "Hey, stop talking about me!" Then
there was my joke about bringing a whole new meaning to the term
"summer outing." *Lay-up*. And when coworkers asked if I would talk
to Big Ed about extending the open bar at the summer outing, I said,
"Look guys, I've got more important things to worry about—like which
bathroom I'm gonna use."

I was only half kidding, actually.

Peeing had become extremely inconvenient. I had promised the
executive board I would wait two weeks before using the men's room
to give people time to adjust to the idea of me being in there, but I
couldn't use the ladies' room either. So every time I had to go, I took
the fourteenth-floor elevator down to the lobby, headed out the back
entrance, and walked two blocks to Rebecca's Café, where there was a
one-person unisex bathroom. Initially I felt obligated to buy something
each time, but seeing that my bladder was the size of a grape, I realized
I'd go broke. So I limited my fluid intake, which cut my bathroom trips
down to three a day.

After the two weeks were up, I headed to the men's room on my
floor and . . . walked right past it after seeing two guys already on their

way in. I guess the board had a point: If I wasn't ready to be in there with my male coworkers, why should they be ready for me?

I made a lap around the floor and killed a few minutes. When I approached the men's room door again, the coast was clear and thankfully, once inside, I had the place to myself. Looking around, I couldn't figure out what all the fuss was about. It was a lot smaller than the ladies' room, and because of the urinals there was space for only two stalls. I chose one of them and closed the door behind me. As soon as I flushed the toilet, I heard the bathroom door open and two male voices in mid-conversation. Then came the sound of unzipping and inevitably, peeing.

I froze. Do I stay in the stall and wait them out? They probably heard the flush, so that might be weird—weirder than seeing me emerge from the stall, anyway. Nope, I'll just go out there and act like it's no big deal. That's what a guy would do. I opened the door and took a step out toward the sinks.

I could tell who the guys were just by looking at their backs; I knew them but wasn't really friends with them. Remembering that bar mitzvah card about urinal etiquette, I didn't expect either of them to take their eyes off the wall they were facing, but one of them turned his head to see who the surprise guest was and, upon discovering it was me, immediately fell silent. This caused the other guy to look in my direction and then suddenly they both stopped talking and followed urinal etiquette to the letter. Now the only sound in the men's room was the running water from the sink I was using. I literally scared the piss out of them—or *into* them; they held the rest of their pee until I left. Whatever. I had christened the fourteenth-floor men's room and was brimming with confidence—until the next time I went in that day.

It was just before noon, and I hadn't yet learned that was the worst time to go to the men's room if you're looking for some privacy. I had just gotten out of a meeting and had been holding my pee for the better part of an hour. I burst through the door about to burst myself and, as it swung closed behind me, stopped dead in my tracks: Both urinals were taken with one guy waiting for his turn; both sinks were being used; and a big pair of feet, pants draped around the ankles, was visible beneath the first stall. Luckily, the door to the other stall was ajar, signaling it was free. I was flustered but refused to let it show. I wanted to prove to everyone that I was as comfortable in this room as they were. So I strode confidently over to the vacant stall and yanked the door open with purpose, only to find Ron, King of the Creative Department, sitting on the throne with a surprised look on his face.

Mortified, I closed the door as quickly as I'd opened it. Also being the master of the one-liner, Ron summed up the situation perfectly with, "What are the odds?" But all I could hear was the laughter as I fled, leaving both my confidence and dignity behind.

After my next meeting, I booked it over to Hank's, a dive bar and secret lunch place where Mary, Sheila, and I met when Mary needed a Scotch & Coke to help get her through the day. I slid a broken wooden chair up to the lopsided table while my coworkers took the first sips of their drinks. I didn't have to say a word. They could tell something was up by the look on my face.

"What's wrong, dee-ah?" Mary asked in her Scottish brogue.

"Oh, nothing much. I just walked in on Ron on the toilet."

"We know." Sheila laughed.

"What?!"

"Brett told us! He was in the men's room when it happened."

Brett! I should've known when I saw him in there. Word of this incident had surely spread through both the fourteenth and thirteenth floors by now and that was just . . . fine. I had to laugh. My second time in the men's room and I walk in on the chief creative officer taking care of business. As Ron so eloquently put it, what were the odds?

When I returned to the agency I got some good-natured ribbing and a slap on the back from Ron. It was as though I'd passed some kind of initiation. Over the next few days, I was in and out of the men's room like I owned the place, knowing if I had a sense of humor about it, so would everyone else. Just like Bet said.

LET THE TRANSITION BEGIN

Summer 1995

I walked into the Newbury Street salon with a Nautica ad in my pocket and the usual knot in my stomach. The reason for the ad was the male model had a haircut I liked. The reason for the knot was I was about to ask my stylist, Kate, to give me that haircut.

Some people going through this transition probably would've taken the easy way out and just gone somewhere else. The thought crossed my mind, but Kate was by far the best stylist I'd ever had. My hairstyle wasn't complicated; there wasn't a name for it or anything. It was short (for a girl) and pretty nondescript. The problem was I couldn't describe the haircut I truly wanted. I tried that once, the first time my mom took Wendy and me to an official hair "salon" in fourth grade. The stylist asked me how I wanted my hair cut, and I didn't know how to answer so I said "like him" and pointed to the man styling the woman's hair in the chair across from me. Wendy burst out laughing and then my mom and the stylist quietly negotiated some hairdo I hated. From then on, I just gave stylists parameters, they'd ignore them, do whatever they wanted, and I'd leave unhappy. Kate really listened and asked a lot of questions to make sure I'd like what she did. I decided it was in my best interest to add her to my hit list.

"Okay Kris, what are we doing today?" she asked, fastening the smock around my neck. "Same as usual?"

"Um . . . no. Something different this time."

"Oh, okay." She looked at me, smiling, waiting for elaboration.

"I . . . um . . ." *Oh no.* I could feel my eyes welling up.

Why is it with some people I can tell my story without getting emotional but with others I can't hold back the tears?

Sensing this was likely going to be a delicate conversation, Kate brought me around to the other side of the mirror partition for some privacy. Soon she too had tears in her eyes but after a quick hug, got right down to business and asked me what I was thinking. I reached into my back pocket and handed her the ad I'd torn out of *GQ*. Kate gave it a quick once-over, evaluated the style—longer on the top, shorter on the sides, a bit messy in the front—and suggested approaching the cut in two stages. She didn't want to go too short right away. Neither did I; I didn't want to go into work and shock people. My goal was to handle the physical aspects of my transition gradually to give people a chance to get used to the new me. To achieve this I needed to avoid drastic changes that might give the agency gossip mill something to talk about.

While she snipped away and gave me a shorter, more decidedly masculine haircut, I noticed the receptionist and a few other stylists who had seen me coming in for the last few years, stealing curious glances at me through the mirror. I didn't care. Because while Kate was using the clippers on the back of my neck, I took a good look at my reflection and actually smiled. For the first time in my life the person staring back at me was starting to look familiar.

Empowered by my new haircut, I went straight home and straight to my bedroom. I had an old-school closet—the kind with two sliding doors that overlapped each other on a track. On the left side were all the clothes I liked to wear, mostly men's Ralph Lauren button-downs and polo shirts, sweaters, and sweatshirts. Behind the right-hand closet door, which had a broken runner and was therefore more challenging to open, I kept all the creepy female clothes I had to wear for formal occasions. I hated opening that damned door. But not this time. This time, I was armed with a black Hefty garbage bag. So long, skirts! Buh-bye, black dress! Suck it, heels! The Goodwill trailer is waiting for your sorry asses.

Next I moved on to my drawers. Literally. I threw out all my underwear. Nothing gave me more pleasure than chucking those bras. I couldn't have my breasts removed (or any other irreversible procedure) until I'd proven to my therapist that I could live full-time in my male role for six months, so until then I had to bind them. Luckily my boobs were relatively small. A classic Ace bandage did the trick. Binding wasn't pleasant, especially when transitioning over the summer, but it gave me the appearance of having a flat male chest and felt more masculine than strapping on a bra. Finally, I searched every other drawer and chucked any item of clothing that came from the women's department.

It was one of the happiest, most gratifying moments of my life, but the best was yet to come: Now that I looked the part, I was finally able to shop in a men's store and buy whatever I wanted without feeling self-conscious or embarrassed. Well, until I'd have to hand over my credit card and any sales person paying attention would see the name Kristin . . . I'd deal with that later. For now, clothes would maketh the man. I stocked up on Calvin Klein boxers and picked up a few dress shirts and ties. I never would have thought wearing something knotted around my neck could feel so liberating.

Speaking of liberation, the next morning while in the shower a new realization hit me: I would never have to shave my legs or armpits ever again. Then out of habit I went to blow-dry my hair and realized that thanks to my new haircut, I wouldn't need to do that either. My transition wasn't just making me feel alive; it was buying me thirty minutes of extra sleep!

I left my North End apartment with a spring in my step and set off on my fifteen-minute walk to work. I was sweating a bit with the Ace bandage on but I didn't care. I was still high off my morning epiphanies when I entered the homeless zone of Boston's Downtown Crossing. The usual suspects were in their usual places, including the tall, thin dude with the scraggly beard on the corner of Washington and Summer Street yelling, "Spare-Change-News-pa-per!" in my face. I gave him a buck and smiled.

"Thank-you-sir," he shouted back melodically.

I stopped dead in my tracks. *Holy shit, I pass!* Granted, the observer was a borderline-crazy homeless person, but still, I took it as a good sign—and it was.

I was definitely being seen as a man because all of a sudden I was *invisible.* I was used to men making eye contact with me and often smiling, but now men looked right past me. Turns out, as a short, pubescent-looking guy, I wasn't getting checked out by *anyone*—male or female. In fact, I found that at times women went out of their way to avoid me. I'd be walking home from a night out and find that if I got within ten feet of a girl walking by herself, she would pick up her pace and cross the street to distance herself from me. The first time this happened, I had just come from a fajita joint with notoriously bad ventilation that makes everyone who walks out of there smell like BO, so I rationalized it away. But it kept happening no matter where I was coming from. I was starting to take it personally until I realized what was going on. Now that girls were viewing me as a guy, they were also viewing me as a potential threat (e.g., mugger or rapist). This bothered me at first, but then I totally understood: I too had felt more vulnerable as a girl. Maybe I was actually safer now that I was a guy.

That safety, however, didn't protect me from getting hit in the face with quite a few doors. Before my transition, people were apparently only holding the door for me because I was a woman, not out of common courtesy as I had assumed. And it wasn't just men. Women too. I realized this when a woman entered a department store in front of me and just let the heavy glass door swing shut behind her. I was completely caught off guard and walked into it face first. I mentioned this phenomenon to a fellow writer as he held the door for me on our way out of a client meeting. He laughed and told me some people just don't have any manners regardless of whether they're male or female. He then informed me that if I'm with a woman at a revolving door, the gentlemanly thing to do is to enter first and get it going so she doesn't have to exert any effort.

This guy was a true gentleman in every sense of the word, which is exactly what I intended to be. And as I learned when I was little, getting others to see me as one would require a lot more than just new clothes and a new haircut. For starters, I needed to enforce the use of new pronouns.

For the first two or three years of my transition, I was a correction Nazi. If you referred to me as "she," I'd say "he" before you could finish your next word. Bet actually prescribed this behavior, warning me not to let it slide when people made mistakes. "Correct them gently but right when it happens," she said. "They need to know you're serious about this change and that they, in turn, need to take your change seriously. The more outs you give people, the longer it will take them to unlearn their old behavior." So I had let people know at the office not to get flustered if I corrected them and that I understood it would take some time to break old habits.

This proved to be more challenging for my family, particularly Wendy, because out of everyone, she spent the most time with me. At one point when I corrected her she snapped.

"Stop correcting me!"

"I know it's aggravating," I said, "but my therapist says I have to."

"Well, at least give me a chance to correct myself before you jump in."

Fair enough. I could tell she was frustrated. But so was I. People don't realize how degrading it is for a trans person to be called by the wrong pronoun—especially in front of other people. I remember early in my transition I was with a girl I had a crush on and when we ran into Wendy she said, "Helloooo, ladies." I winced, causing her to quickly add "and gentlemen." But it was too late. The damage had been done. Afterward she apologized profusely and I accepted, knowing it wasn't intentional.

But what I couldn't understand was why two years later, when there was essentially nothing female about my appearance left, these pronoun slipups were still happening. Not with friends and coworkers, *just* my family. I brought this up with Bet at my next therapy session. She reminded me that I'd been a daughter and sister to my family for twenty-six years before I transitioned.

"Imagine if you died," Bet said. "How long do you think it would take your family to get over mourning you?"

"I don't know . . . a long time."

"Think they'd be over it in two years and ready to move on?"

"No."

"Well, that's what's happening here. They need to mourn the loss of their daughter and sister before they can fully let go and accept you as a son and brother. You've been talking about Wendy and your parents—you even mention your grandmother slipping up a lot. I haven't heard you mention Jill yet. Is she making pronoun mistakes too?"

"No. Not really. But I don't see her as much."

"More than your grandmother, though."

"Yeah."

"So why do you think Jill doesn't have a problem getting the pronouns right?"

"Well . . . she did say she always thought of me more as a brother than a sister."

"And I remember you telling me Jill was the most accepting when you first told your family. She said, 'I'd rather have you as a brother than not at all.'"

"Yeah, she did."

"So she's probably not mourning the loss of her sister like Wendy is. Just be patient. They'll all get there in their own time."

Bet was right, of course. At Sunday dinner when Wendy and Mom simultaneously pounced on poor Gram for incorrectly referring to me as "her," I became much more optimistic. Now if they could just get her to stop calling me Kristin . . .

WHAT'S IN A NAME?

Summer 1995

If you think naming a child is hard, try naming yourself. Or in my case *renaming*, which is even tougher because you're asking people to unlearn something and adopt something new instead of starting from scratch. As anyone in advertising will tell you, changing consumer habits is a challenge, especially when changing perception is part of the assignment. Take J. C. Penney: At one point they changed their name to "JCP" in an effort to "hip up" their image. It didn't stick because it didn't fit their brand. My goal was for everyone to see me as a guy, so I needed a guy's name—but it had to be one that fit *me*.

My first name was a no-brainer. I was born "Kristin," but people called me Kris, which I really liked, so I decided to change my full name to Christopher and still go by Chris. This made it easy for everyone. Well, almost everyone. While my family called me Kris and a slew of other nicknames, they also sometimes called me Kristin, so they did have a little unlearning to do. But hey, it could've been worse. As my boss, Ron, put it after hearing the news, "I'm just glad he didn't change his name to Frank." (By the way, I feel it's worth noting here you should never ask a transgender person what their birth name was. While it may seem like a harmless question, it is hurtful because you are reminding them of the gender identity they are purposely trying to leave behind and likely bringing back painful memories. Plus, it's really none of your business.)

When it came to changing my last name, I wavered back and forth. Part of me wanted to change it as a way of moving forward in my new identity, but the other part of me didn't because I felt like I'd be giving up both my family name and my Armenian heritage. My sisters planned on changing their names when they got married, so they suggested I keep it so Dad's name would live on. My mom agreed with them. When I talked to my father about it, he said whatever I wanted to do was okay by him and that he'd understand if I wanted to change it. But something in his tone made me feel that deep down he was hoping I'd keep it. I was torn. After a few weeks of weighing the pros and cons, I told my family I was going to change my last name and outlined the reasons why.

First, "Eskandarian" is unique, and I worried it might make things difficult or awkward for me during my transition. Say I met someone who knew one of my sisters somehow. I could see the conversation playing out as follows:

Hey, I know an Eskandarian. Are you related to Wendy?

Yeah, I'm her brother.

Huh . . . I thought she had two sisters.

Or say I'm at a party and get introduced to someone who may have known me from high school or something. I could hear it now:

Hey, Laura, this is Chris Eskandarian. He grew up in Wayland too.

Oh, I knew a Kris Eskandarian a couple grades ahead of me. But she was a girl. That's weird . . .

See where I'm going with this?

Second, changing my last name would help me build my professional reputation independent of my father. I was already uncomfortable with clients and vendors automatically knowing I was the CEO's kid and felt the whole nepotism thing was undermining my credibility as a legit writer.

Finally, having a new last name signaled a fresh start for me. I told my family it was a tough decision, but I felt it was the right one, adding that if I ever wanted to reclaim my original last name, I could always change it back. They were all on board, though my dad looked a little sad behind the eyes. Then, Jill blurted out the obvious question, "Well? What are you changing it to?"

I told them I wanted it to still begin with the letter "E" and waited for them to guess. They stared at me blankly. When I said "Edwards" they all smiled. It was a pseudonym we'd always used when calling restaurants to make reservations or to order pizza or something, simply because it was easier than having to spell out E-s-k-a-n-d . . . We'd been using it for so long everyone seemed to have forgotten that its origin was my father's name. Since I wasn't using his last, I wanted to use his first.

Then I told them the other reason why I chose it—a conversation that had stuck with me since I was eleven years old. It happened during one of our six-hour station wagon rides to visit my dad's side of the family in Telford, Pennsylvania. To help pass the time, Mom was telling us how my grandfather, Pop Pop, was upset when he first found out his new granddaughter's name was Wendy. He had never heard such a name before and couldn't pronounce it: "*Vindy? Vhat is Vindy?*" Then Dad chimed in and told Jill they almost named her "Catherine" after Grammom and that "Jill" was going to be her middle name so they could call her "CJ." This information did not go over well with Jill. Turned out she liked her "almost name" better than the one she ended up with.

"What about me?" I asked from the way back. "What was my name gonna be?" After a beat of silence, my mom answered.

"Edward," she said craning her neck toward the back seat. "The doctor told us we were having a boy, so we were going to name you 'Edward' after Dad. There were no accurate tests back then. But I really thought you were gonna be a boy too—it felt different than when I was carrying Wendy."

I put my Walkman headphones back on and stewed, *I knew it! The doctor even thought I was supposed to be a boy. What the hell???*

When I finished recounting the story everyone looked freaked out, especially Mom. She had forgotten all about it until I brought it up. She said she thought something hormonal must have happened while I was in the womb and that she strongly believed the theory in the literature she read about changes in brain chemistry being the cause of gender dysphoria.

"Okay, well, what about your middle name?" Jill asked, changing the subject and bringing us all back to the present.

I told them I wanted my initials to spell CRE (another family nickname, which at the time was spelled KRE) and that I chose Ryan because it was a name I liked that began with "R." Nothing deeper than that.

"So," I said, "Christopher Ryan Edwards. There you have it."

But I didn't have it, yet. The process was just beginning.

••

I jogged up the steps of the Suffolk County Courthouse and found my way to the Probate and Family Court Department, where I explained to an extremely crotchety clerk that I was changing my name and needed to file the appropriate paperwork.

"There's a fee," she barked, handing me a form, "and we only take cash."

"No problem," I said.

"I'll need your birth certificate and marriage license."

Crap. She thinks I'm a woman. I should've worn a tie and lowered my voice to sound more like a guy.

"I'm not married," I said, in my deepest register.

"Then why are you changing your name?"

"Uh . . ."

As if on cue, an angel of mercy appeared—a woman in her late thirties with the air of a helpful librarian. She cut in with impeccable timing, preventing me from having to answer.

"Are you changing your *full* name?" she asked.

"Yes."

"Okay, that process is a bit more complicated. You'll need to fill out this change of name petition with your birth name. Fill in the name you're changing it to here and the reason for the change."

I looked at her nervously.

Just then the phone rang. The crotchety clerk snatched up the receiver and from what I could tell was just as unhelpful to the caller as she was to me.

The angel said softly, "Fill out the paperwork over there, come back when you're done, and I'll help you." She smiled and I smiled back, relieved. *She must know.*

As I filled out the form with "CC" still barking on the phone in the background, I wondered which fixture had been in this office longer: the chain attached to the pen I was using, or her. Either way, I was selfishly relieved someone else was now suffering in my place. I tuned her out and focused all my attention on the form.

Name at Present: *Kristin Lynne Eskandarian*
(Ugh, I hated how it rhymed.)
To be changed to: *Christopher Ryan Edwards*
Ever changed name before? *No*
Reason for change: *Gender Reassignment*

I signed it, dated it, and back to the counter I went. The angel looked over the form and asked for my birth certificate and the filing fee. She stamped the form, disappeared for a few minutes, and then came back with instructions.

"Okay, so you'll need to publish your name change in the newspaper . . ."

Say what now?

". . . then after thirty days, bring a copy of the newspaper announcement back here and we'll set a court date and get you in front of the judge."

I stood there stupefied. I was expecting this to be official today and was NOT expecting to have to publish my name change in the freaking newspaper.

"I have to announce this in the newspaper?"

"Yes, it's an obligatory procedure everyone has to do to make sure you're not changing your name to defraud anyone or get out of debts you might owe," Angel explained.

"Oh."

Sensing my discomfort, she then leaned in closer and whispered some conspiratorial advice. "It doesn't have to be *The Boston Globe*. You can publish it in any paper."

"*Any* paper?"

"Any paper."

By the end of the following week, news of my name change was published in the legal notices section of the *Post-Gazette* or, as it was known then, *La Gazzetta del Massachusetts—The Italian-American Voice of Massachusetts*. Next time you're in Boston's North End, see if you can dig up a copy. It comes out once a week. On Fridays.

Grazie, Angel.

Thirty days later I was back at the courthouse, this time wearing a tie and clutching the page from the *Post-Gazette*. I scanned behind the Probate and Family counter for Angel. She wasn't there. Crotchety Clerk was there in full force, but thankfully she was tied up making someone else's life miserable, so another woman came over to help me. I gave her my docket number along with the required newspaper clipping and she pulled up my file. I watched her process it physically and mentally. Based on her eyes and expression, I was ninety-five percent sure she would be sympathetic.

"Do you have to be somewhere?" she asked. "I mean, can you wait around for an hour, hour and a half?"

"Ah, yeah if I need to, sure."

"Okay, good. Reason I ask is because there's another judge due here in an hour or so who would be more *sensitive* than the one presiding now. I think you'd be better off to wait if you can."

Looks like God sent me another angel.

"Thank you so much. I will definitely wait."

"Okay, have a seat on the bench and I'll come get you when it's time."

I sat there out in the hall, stunned and grateful. I was not expecting this kind of treatment—really just the opposite. As promised, Angel No. 2 reappeared ninety minutes later and walked me to the courtroom, prepping me along the way. She let me know that she'd already spoken to the judge about my "special circumstance" and told me that when he calls my name, I should walk right up to the bench to talk to him—not stand up at the podium across the room like everyone else. He wanted to handle my case privately and not embarrass me in front of an entire courtroom full of people.

I couldn't believe this woman did all that for me. I was so overwhelmed with gratitude that when we got to the courtroom door, I gave her a huge hug, which caught her completely off guard. She hugged me back and wished me luck.

Inside the courtroom, I waited with approximately forty others for my turn with the judge. After about ten minutes, he called my name and motioned for me to approach the bench, leaving everyone else to wonder what was so special about me. He was in his mid-fifties, conservative looking, and impeccably groomed. His black robe combined with wire-rimmed glasses and perfectly parted graying hair made him seem extremely judicial, and despite what Angel No. 2 had told me, I still found myself intimidated by him. As he spoke to me though, the stern tone he'd had during the former proceedings softened and became more fatherly. After a few formalities, he asked me one question: Was I changing my name for purposes of fraud?

"No, sir."

He signed the document, smiled, and said, "Good luck, Christopher."

••

The following Friday was another August scorcher. It was also my day off. Normally I'd be on my way to the Cape instead of the Registry of Motor Vehicles, but I was a man with a mission: Now that my name change was legal, I could officially change it on my driver's license. The big question was could I change the "F" that was on there to an "M"? Bet had warned me this might be an issue and gave me a document from the State Registrar's Office that basically said anyone going through gender reassignment in the state of Massachusetts could have the gender designation left blank on their driver's license. I asked about this at one of my F-to-M support group meetings and got mixed responses. One guy used the Registrar's letter and had his sex left blank. A couple of the guys said they didn't have the letter at the time and were stuck with Fs on their licenses. Another guy said he got an M without having to show the letter. Bottom line: It was a crapshoot—totally depended on who you got at the window. I'd had pretty good luck at the courthouse so I was feeling optimistic. I strode confidently into the RMV in my khakis, loafers, and repp tie, looking like Mr. Preppy. Best-case scenario: I'd leave with an M on my license. Worst case: I'd have my sex left blank. Either way, I was leaving there without an effing F.

I entered the stale, cavernous waiting area, took a number (64), grabbed a seat, and sized up the situation at the service counter. There were nine windows. Eight were open and manned by inner-city kids who looked like they were just out of high school and would rather be anywhere but this place. *Good. Maybe they won't be paying attention or won't care and will just give me the M. They might look at me like I'm a freak, but whatever, I'll deal with it. Whoa, wait a minute. Where did SHE come from?*

Fresh off her lunch break, in waddled Old Mother Hen. Early sixties and bossy, she was clearly the supervisor—shouting orders, yelling out numbers, and chastising both employees and patrons for not paying attention. To my horror, she filled the last vacant window. I could tell by her demeanor and the glasses on the chain around her neck that she'd be a stickler for the rules: my nemesis.

Still, nine-to-one odds said I'd get somebody else. As numbers in the high fifties started being called, I began my internal chant: *Not her. Not her. Not her.* And then I heard that unmistakable shrill.

"Sixty-fo-wah!"

Son of a . . . !

I got up from my chair and headed over to her window . . .

"Sixty-fo-wah!"

. . . clearly not fast enough for her liking. In the deepest voice I could muster I told her I needed to change my name on my license then handed over my old license and the court document bearing my new name. (I kept the letter from the state registrar in my pocket but was prepared to use it if I had to.) She glanced at the items quickly, typed something into her computer, and then gave me my marching orders.

"Okay, fella, go stand in line for your picture. Your license will come out over there. When it's ready they'll call your name."

"Ah, okay. Thank—"

"Seventy-one!"

"—you."

When it was my turn, I took my place in front of the blue backdrop, which I noticed was almost the same color as my shirt. *Damn it!* I was barely in position when the flash went off and I was told to move on. *Double damn it!* After a few minutes I heard the girl manning the laminate machine call out "Christopha Edwuhds."

It took a second for me to register that it was my name she was calling. No one had ever called me by it before—let alone in a thick Boston accent. I trotted over to get my new license. The anticipation was killing me but I was afraid to look. When I saw the picture I was relieved. It wasn't as bad as I feared. My eyes were open and I didn't look constipated or anything. I scanned my name. It was spelled right, and under "sex" there was indeed a letter.

F.

As in *Fuck!*

License in hand, I trudged back over to the dreaded window. I was sweating now. Not sure if it was the lack of AC, the Ace bandage around my chest, or my nerves, but I wiped my palms on my pant legs and pulled Plan B out of my pocket. As soon as Old Mother Hen finished with seventy-nine, I stepped up before she could call the next number.

"Hi . . . um this . . . " With no plan in place for what I was going to say, I just handed her my license and pointed to the F.

Great, I was a mime now.

She pulled on her glasses to take a closer look.

"Huh, how did that get there?" she said, confused. "Sorry, Hun, I'll take care of that." She typed something into the computer and sent me back to the laminating machine. I slowly walked over there in shock. *Did that really just happen?*

Yup.

Hello M!

••

With luck on my side and a new driver's license in my wallet, I headed over to the Social Security Office to get a new card. Surprisingly, that step proved to be the least difficult and most uneventful. I was in and out of there in fifteen minutes. I was officially on a roll and onto my last stop. The U.S. Passport Agency.

After twenty minutes of waiting in a line that moved like a boa constrictor slowly strangling its prey, I ended up at the window of a friendly looking gentleman with sandy-colored hair and outdated glasses. He reminded me of my seventh-grade math teacher.

"Can I help you?" he asked cheerfully.

Sweet! Another nice person. I deepened my voice: "Yes, hi, I changed my name so I need a new passport."

I handed him my application complete with the two-inch by two-inch photos I'd had taken a few days earlier.

"Do you have your old passport?"

"Yes, and here's all my other stuff," I said, handing over my court document, new license, and social security card.

He read the court document, looked a bit confused, and then opened up my old passport. He stared at the picture of me taken when I was seventeen, then at my license, then at me, and then his confused expression turned to disgust.

I was no longer prepared for this, not after my previous positive experiences. That one look he gave me completely shattered my self-esteem. On the inside, I was crumbling. On the outside, I stood there like a statue, head held high, while he called his supervisor over to discuss the situation. He said something to her that I couldn't hear, and then pointed at me. I stared right back at them both. The supervisor read over the documents and told him it was legal.

He refused to wait on me.

The supervisor gave me an embarrassed look, took my cash, and said she'd be right back. Ten minutes later she returned with a receipt and the promise that my new passport would arrive in four to six weeks. I thanked her and got the hell out of there. I couldn't wait to get to the Cape.

Four weeks later, my passport arrived. I proudly showed it to my mom, who thought I looked handsome in my picture. But what was more pleasing to my eyes was the big fat "M" under "sex/sexe/sexo." This was a huge bonus because, as I later found out, to legally change the sex designation on any of my documentation, I was supposed to supply an affidavit from a doctor indicating that I had undergone irreversible gender reassignment surgery (for F-to-Ms, a mastectomy is usually enough). The fact that I changed my name to Christopher and had begun living full-time as a man technically wasn't enough. So when it came to changing my birth certificate, I decided not to push my luck; I waited nine months until I had the affidavit, then headed to the city hall in Revere, the town of the hospital where I was born.

Compared to Boston's City Hall, this place was more like "City Small" and the Clerk's office was only a tad larger than my father's. There were two people behind the counter, both in their late twenties. I stood there patiently while they pretended not to notice me. After a throat clear and an "Excuse me," one of them finally made eye contact, and in the stereotypical Boston accent out-of-staters expect everyone from Massachusetts to have, begrudgingly asked if he could help me.

"Yes, I need to change my name and gender on my birth certificate."

He just stared at me, squinting. I braced myself.

"Yuh whut?"

"Need to change the name and gender on my birth certificate," I repeated. "Here's all the documentation and the fee, plus twenty dollars for two copies."

He stared at me like I was the most repulsive human being he had ever laid eyes on, and I stared right back, stone-faced, daring him to question me. He shook his head, half-whispered something degrading about me to his female counterpart, and then they both enjoyed a good laugh at my expense. Oddly, it didn't sting as much as the incident at the Passport Agency. Maybe because I expected this kind of behavior from these two bozos, and the passport guy caught me off guard because he was older—fatherly—and nice to me until he put it all together. Or maybe I was just gaining more inner strength.

I pondered all this while the two of them disappeared behind a side door I hadn't noticed existed. After fifteen minutes or so, the guy came back out. He slapped the new documents down on the counter without saying a word, quickly pulling his hand away so as not to catch any of my "disease," and then turned his back to me.

I grabbed the certificates and headed for the door also without saying a word. Okay, I might have muttered "*Thanks, fuckface*" under my breath, but not before making sure my new name was spelled correctly and that next to "sex" it said "male" and not something wise-ass like "Yes, please."

It took almost a full year before I finally got all my documentation changed over. And by then, a lot of other things about me had changed too.

TESTOSTERONE POWER

September 1995

I was at Boston Medical Center about to take the first step toward my irreversible physical transformation: testosterone injections, which I'd need to have every two weeks for the rest of my life. I wasn't sure if I'd actually get one at my first appointment, but I knew from my support group that when it came to endocrinologists, Dr. Chipkin was "the man" and that he and his staff were very supportive of transgender patients. This put me at ease, which was a good thing, seeing that my last visit with an endocrinologist had left me totally traumatized.

It was my sophomore year in high school, and Mom was taking me to see a doctor who, she told me, might be able to adjust my hormone levels so I wouldn't be so hairy. The doctor came highly recommended by one of Mom's best friends. I was curious why Wendy wasn't coming with us (we both bleached our Armo mustaches), but I never asked. Deep down I always knew I was different from her. Maybe Mom did too.

She waited with me in the ice-cold exam room, while I sat shivering in my paper robe. When the doctor finally arrived, she forced my mom out into the waiting room despite both our requests that she stay. This kicked my predilection for worry into overdrive. *What was this woman going to do to me?* I sized her up as she ushered Mom out of the room and closed the door: medium height, heavyset, with straight salt-and-pepper hair, big glasses, and a nose shaped like a parrot's. Her voice was loud and abrasive. Even louder was the voice inside my head shouting, *Run!*

She asked me a bunch of questions: When did I first get my period? *Age twelve.* Was I sexually active? *No.* Did my father ever touch me inappropriately? *WHAT?* Then she briefly examined me in a place where I'd never been examined before and after a few seconds stopped and announced, "Your clitoris is fine!" As I struggled to comprehend what that meant for me, she opened the door and yelled the great news to someone else out in the hallway. I was mortified, confused, and humiliated. She closed the door, came back over to me, and said, "You're not a man!" adding that I should see a psychiatrist and so should my mother.

Too stunned to say anything, I got dressed and found Mom in the waiting room. She could tell something was wrong and once outside the office asked me what the doctor said. I burst into tears and told her. She was furious and told me to forget we ever came here. On the ride home, I wondered why the doctor would have said anything about my thinking I was a man. Did Mom think I was? Did she say something to her friend who said something to the doctor when setting up the appointment? Was the hairy thing just a ruse to get me to agree to go? No matter, I was too traumatized to ask any questions— mostly because I was afraid to know the answers and have to admit to my feelings.

Ten years later, the irony of the current situation was not lost on me: Mom and I, once again waiting to see an endocrinologist, this time to help me become the man we both had secretly suspected I always was.

There are plenty of reasons someone might see an endocrinologist—diabetes, thyroid, anything glandular—so it's not like everyone in the waiting room was necessarily going in for testosterone shots. Still, I found myself sizing up the only other patient there, trying to determine if he, too, was transgender. He pretty much kept his head down and didn't make eye contact, but I noticed, like me, he had relatively small hands and small feet, which as it turns out is a pretty good indicator.

"Do you think he is?" Mom whispered to me, cocking her head in his direction.

I nodded.

A few minutes later, Dr. Chipkin personally came out to greet us and escort us to his office. I liked him immediately. He reminded me of Dennis Franz, the actor who played Andy Sipowicz on NYPD Blue, only slimmer and with better skin and a gentle, easygoing way. He also had a *Star Trek* pin on the lapel of his lab coat, which my mom commented on; he shyly confessed that yes, he was a "Trekkie."

Then the conversation turned to my hormone therapy: biweekly testosterone injections, the dosage of which would be determined by trial and error and blood tests to ensure no harm was being done to my liver. The goal was to settle on the lowest possible dosage to yield the desired results. I naively asked him if he could administer just enough testosterone to grow facial hair, deepen my voice, and build muscle, but not so much that I'd grow back hair or develop male-pattern baldness. (I'd been privy to enough discussions with women to know that neither of those traits were desirable.) He laughed and informed me that there was no way of controlling those variables. If male-pattern baldness and back hair runs in my family, I would have just as much chance of inheriting them as if I had been born a genetic male. Images of Dad's hairy back and the bald uncles on my mother's side popped into my head.

Crap!

I lobbed one more question at him out of desperation: "Is there any chance these hormone injections could make me taller?"

"Sorry," he said. "Your bones stopped growing at around age thirteen."

Double crap!

I made mental notes to do the following:

- Research side effects of Rogaine

- Find a good back-waxer

- Spread the rumor to every girl I know that flats are making a comeback

Dr. Chipkin informed me that I would not be getting an injection at this appointment. Instead I would fill out some forms and go to the lab to have blood drawn, then come back in two weeks for my first shot. I started to fill out the paperwork while my mom engaged him in some small talk. When I got to the question about my sex, I stared at the two boxes marked "male" and "female." Unsure which one I was technically supposed to check at this stage of the game, I turned to Dr. Chipkin.

"Should I put down male?"

He smiled, "Isn't that why we're here?"

••

Two weeks later Mom and I were back in the endocrinology waiting room, this time with Wendy seated between us. They both wanted to be there for my first injection and then go out for dinner afterward to celebrate.

My sister nudged me and motioned to a guy sitting in the corner reading, indicating she thought he might be transgender. I squinted for a closer look and shook my head. Nope. While she scanned the room for more possible suspects, I distracted myself with Cassie, the pretty blonde nurse who came out to get me for my shot. I jumped up, ready to follow her, when Mom grabbed my arm and handed me something heavy wrapped in tissue paper.

"Here, give this to Dr. Chipkin."

"What is it?"

"It's a 'Star Trek' mug. Tell him it's for his desk."

Wendy and I rolled our eyes while Cassie waited patiently. She led me to an exam room where Dr. Chipkin was reviewing my blood test results. After exchanging quick pleasantries, I handed him the mug, embarrassed.

"This is from my mom. She thought you'd like it for your desk."

He opened it up and laughed. "Oh, that's great. Tell her thank you for me." Then it was back to business. "Your blood and liver tests look normal, so we're gonna start at 120 mgs and see how that dosage affects you after a few months. Cassie will give you the injections, and I'll see you every three months or so for the first year or until we nail down the proper dosage. You'll notice your voice changing, acne, body hair where you've never had any before . . . you know, all the great things that come with male puberty."

No, I didn't know. I didn't have any brothers.

As I dropped my pants to receive the first of what could potentially be upward of fifteen hundred injections over my lifetime, most of which I would end up administering myself, I realized I was going to go through puberty all over again; only this time I'd be unable to apply anything I'd learned the first time around. I felt the cold, wet alcohol swab on my right check and braced myself for impending pain, but when the nurse stuck me with the slim twenty-one-gauge needle, I didn't really feel it that much. Two seconds later I pulled up my boxers and headed back out to the waiting room.

Mom and Wendy looked expectantly at me. I didn't feel any different than I did before the testosterone shot but gave them my best Incredible Hulk pose just the same. Seemed like we were all anxious to see results. But no one wanted them faster than I did, especially with my cousin Terry's wedding right around the corner. It would be my first formal event and official debut as a man in front of two hundred of my closest relatives.

••

Standing in front of the full-length mirror on the back of the bedroom door, I looked myself up and down: my first men's suit, navy blue, cuffs slightly breaking over my black monk-strap dress shoes. Mom had helped me with the Ace bandage so my chest was bound extra tight, making it virtually undetectable under my dress shirt, jacket, and tie. I'd had only two testosterone injections so far, which meant aside from my haircut, there weren't any real physical changes in my appearance yet; but my entire extended family on my mom's side was about see me as a man for the first time since my announcement. I felt good, but part of me feared that to them I might just look like a woman in drag.

I went downstairs where Wendy's and Jill's boyfriends were making awkward small talk with my father while my sisters finished getting ready.

"Lookin' good, Shtine!" they said. As I returned the compliment, my sisters came down, beautiful as always, and the "Ooh, Shtinys" began along with the whistling and bum pinching. My mom appeared last as usual, and when she saw me, her eyes welled up with tears. She gave me a kiss but before she could say anything, Dad shoved her toward the door, announcing that thanks to her we were now late. Some things never change.

The two young couples went in one car and I rode with my parents. I was quizzing Mom on who would be there and confirming that everyone in attendance already knew my situation. She said that yes, everybody knew, including my younger cousins. I inquired about close family friends I thought would be there and she confirmed that, yes, they knew too.

As we got closer to the church, I lobbed out one last question. "Gram told Great Gram, right?"

Silence.

"Mom?"

"I don't know."

"What? What do you mean you don't know?"

"Well, Gram and I decided it might be better *not* to tell her. The woman's ninety-five. She probably won't know the difference."

"WHAT?"

"But that doesn't mean someone else didn't tell her. Maybe Aunty Ginny or Uncle Robert said something."

"What am I supposed to say when I see her?"

"Just say 'Hi' and give her a hug. She'll probably think you're Adam or Dana."

Oh great.

Wendy, Jill, and the boyfriends found us in the church parking lot and I immediately relayed what I'd just learned. After a quick huddle, "Operation: Avoid Great Gram" was officially underway. It was quickly aborted, however, when we saw our target heading straight for us. Nowhere to run. Nowhere to hide.

"Hiiii, Great Graaam," we all said in unison.

"Come here, *hokis*." One by one she kissed us, uttering more Armenian terms of endearment with each embrace. Until it was my turn, that is, at which point she reverted back to English.

"Oh my god," she said, laughing nervously and looking around for someone—*anyone*—else to move on to. I looked over at Mom, who was now standing with Gram, both of them rolling their eyes.

"Come on, Shtiny," Jill said, dragging me away, Wendy and the two boyfriends in tow.

"Do you think she knows?" I asked. The jury was still out.

Inside the church, most of my relatives were already seated on the groom's side. I felt good in my suit but as I walked down the aisle with all eyes on me, I couldn't help but wonder if I was really pulling it off. Was this how bridesmaids felt? They rarely get to choose what they wear. At least I got to pick out my suit. Still, when I saw Terry at the altar looking sharp in his tuxedo, I wished this wedding had been black tie.

Ever since my prom I had dreamed of wearing a tux and now that I could, I had been begging for an opportunity. It arrived a year later in the form of an advertising award dinner in honor of my father. The tux was a classic shawl collar model given to me by one of the managing partners at Arnold. He had just bought himself a new one, and since we were roughly the same size, he thought with a few alterations it would fit me pretty well. He was right. After my tailor had worked his magic you'd think that tux had been made for me. The shirt actually was, thanks to a gift certificate my dad gave me to the Custom Shop. And once I put on the black onyx cufflinks and studs, black silk bowtie and cummerbund, and shiny patent leather tuxedo shoes, I took a look in the mirror. *Holy shit! Who let James Bond in here?* On a scale of 1 to 10, I was definitely a 007. And when I strode into the Harvard Club, just one among a sea of penguins, I finally felt like I belonged to a different club—the one I'd been denied entry to since birth.

But that night was a year's worth of confidence away. To get through this wedding, I needed liquid courage. So as soon as we got to the reception, the boyfriends and I headed straight to the bar. After a few quick drinks I was much more at ease. We were sitting with my cousins and having a blast. None of them treated me any differently. Jill and I danced together, which drew a lot of attention, but not as much as when I pulled feisty ol' Aunty Mary out on the floor and attempted to dip her. Later, when we found ourselves back at the "cousins table" for cake, Jill announced she had to go to the bathroom and, out of habit, asked me to go with her. When I told her I couldn't, it took her a moment to realize why. I watched tears form in her eyes as she registered the permanent loss of her former ladies' room buddy, which according to Jill was the only thing that bummed her out about my gender change.

I, on the other hand, was about to face an even bigger bummer that few people would ever need or want to go through a second time: puberty.

●●

It only took a few months before I began noticing the signs of Puberty 2.0. The first was acne—worse than I ever had in high school. Dr. Chipkin said I was just going to have to ride it out, but it was a pretty embarrassing ride down the skincare aisle of CVS; me at age twenty-six battling seventh and eighth graders for the last tube of Oxy10. Yet no topical medication—no matter how much benzoyl peroxide it contained—did the trick.

After a particularly bad breakout, Mom informed me that when my cousin went through puberty he had terrible acne and was prescribed something called Accutane, which cleared it right up. That sounded promising, so I went to see a dermatologist in nearby Brookline who came highly recommended. While waiting in his exam room, I grabbed the pamphlet on Accutane and found myself cringing at the "before" pictures. Yikes! My acne problem was nowhere near as bad as what was depicted in these photographs. *Dear God, please don't let me get bacne!* I began reading about the different dosage levels and figured I'd be at the lowest end of the spectrum. Imagine my surprise when the doctor prescribed the highest dose possible. When I questioned him on it his response was simply, "You want to see results, don't you?" *Okay . . .*

Two months later I got a phone call from my college friend, Hazel. Now in business school, her time was at a premium and she was returning my call from two weeks earlier. I was still half asleep when I picked up the phone and mumbled hello.

"It's Hazel."

"Well, well, well. Look who finally decided to call me back."

"You got ten minutes, go."

I started blinking, partially because I was trying to remember the reason why I'd called her in the first place, but mostly because I was seeing double. I relayed this phenomenon to Hazel.

"Oh my god, you're taking Accutane, right?"

"Yeah?"

"I took that in high school and I stopped because my skin got way too dry."

"Tell me about it." I said through severely chapped lips.

"I think double vision is one of the side effects. You better call the doctor and have him lower your dosage."

After my ten minutes with Hazel were up, I checked the pamphlet that came with my medication. *Stop using Acccutane and call your doctor at once if you experience any of the following side effects: blah, blah, blah, blurred or double vision, blah, blah, blah.* I immediately called the doctor's office and explained my situation to the receptionist. She put me on hold and then after a few minutes informed me that I'd have to find another dermatologist as mine was no longer seeing patients. *What the . . . ?*

Since I only had a month left on the meds to go, I decided to just cut my dose in half. Soon my double vision disappeared and thirty days later so did my acne. What did appear though, was this headline in *The Boston Globe*: "Missing Drug Records Cost Brookline Dermatologist His License."

Then there was the hair growth. The only body part I'd be shaving now would be my acne-free face, so per advice from every guy I knew, I chucked all the disposable razors I'd been using on my legs and splurged on the fourteen-dollar Gillette Sensor Excel with the overpriced replaceable cartridges. I was finally taking part in the ritual I had been looking forward to my whole life, cutting myself twice in the process. I was now a member of the club.

At first I couldn't understand why guys complained so much about shaving; it only took like ten minutes, big deal. Try shaving your legs, pits, and bikini line. Shaving your face is nothing. I actually looked forward to it. I loved the fact that I could alter my appearance so easily. I tried out the Elvis sideburns and sported the obligatory goatee, which I shaved down to a mustache right before flying to London with Hazel, just to irritate her. I did the soul patch thing for a hot minute and then went clean shaven. After a few years the thrill wore off and the ritual became a chore, which is exactly what every guy had pretty much told me would happen. I stopped shaving altogether and grew a beard—another male rite of passage (and a piece of cake for an Armenian guy)—but that got too itchy and I got rid of it in time for the summer. I ended up settling on the scruff thing, shaving maybe once a week and before flights to avoid being profiled as a terrorist.

In addition to my face, hair was also sprouting up on other parts of my body like my chest, my back (although not as badly as I'd feared), and my ass, which was a lovely surprise. The hair on my arms and legs grew longer and coarser. The hair on my head, however, not so much. My hairline began to recede around the temples and my forehead widened, giving me a squarer, more masculine look. I didn't really notice the transformation while it was happening, but it is striking when I look back at pictures of myself during that five-year period I call "The Great Recession." Eventually, when the handfuls of hair started coming out in the shower, I got so depressed I hit the bottle. The Propecia bottle.

The other hairy situation was my voice. The female register was a dead giveaway, especially on the phone when the person on the other end didn't have any visual clues to pair it with. I was really looking forward to the testosterone working its magic in that department. The doctor said my voice would get deeper but I honestly didn't know what to expect; girls' voices just don't change in the same way.

The first time it happened I was on a conference call with my team presenting ads to a client. The eight of us were taking turns shouting into a regular old office phone that we'd put on speaker. The art director had just finished going over the print, and I was now performing the radio spots I'd written, doing my best to bring the characters to life. I was on a roll until I tried to hit a high note and my voice cracked. I was completely caught off guard, as was everyone else in the room. They had all been on this transformation journey with me, learning as I went, but this was something new if not unfamiliar to the other guys in the room. I excused myself and forged on, picking up where I'd left off. I thought I was in the clear when I got to the announcer section, but on "*Hurry in*" I croaked again, this time to audible laughter.

"Who let that frog in here?" I joked. My client, also aware of my transition, laughed too and asked me if I needed to gargle before presenting the next spot.

For months it continued: mid-word, mid-sentence, and often at the most inopportune moments. At presentations, bets were placed on whether or not I'd make it through a script without my voice cracking, the over/under based on how many female characters there were in a spot. Soon I earned the nickname "Peter Brady" in honor of one of the classic episodes of "The Brady Bunch" when Peter's voice changes. As the song from the show goes, "When it's time to change you've got to rearrange . . . who you are and what you're gonna be."

Eventually my voice deepened into the high end of the male register. I was being mistaken for a woman on the phone less and less and had virtually no problems passing in person. I did develop another problem that I wasn't expecting, though. All of a sudden I was snoring like a freight train. I'd doze off on the couch and everyone would yell that they couldn't hear the TV. If I crashed at a friend's place, I'd drive everyone out of the room because my snoring was so bad. I had never snored in my life so I found this extremely disturbing. I went to see a specialist, who after examining me said that because the testosterone had thickened my larynx and vocal cords, the opening in my throat had become roughly fifty percent smaller. He also noted that my tonsils were enlarged but couldn't say for certain if that was due to the hormones. Regardless, they needed to come out to give me a larger airway to breathe through, and hopefully that would stop the snoring or at least decrease it.

Let me tell you this: Out of all the surgeries I'd end up enduring, the tonsillectomy ranks in the top three for most painful recovery. On the upside, it reduced my snoring by about eighty percent, and I lost seven pounds, which proved to be a much-needed bonus.

Like most guys on testosterone, I gained weight. A ton of weight. Seriously, people always told me I was "tons of fun," but now it was a cold, hard fact. Part of the gain came from the steroids adding bulk and inducing cravings for red meat. But part of it was my own fault: I was eating french fries with every meal and my idea of exercise was walking to the refrigerator and back. I gained thirty pounds in that first year, going from a waist 32 to a waist 36. For someone just under 5'4," that was huge (as was my ass). That summer, I went for my annual physical and when the nurse weighed me in at 167 pounds, I almost fell off the scale. *How did I get this way? Why hadn't anyone said anything to me? There should've been an intervention!*

My primary care doctor sat me down for a serious talk, not only about my weight but also about my cholesterol level. She explained that it had already been elevated because of the testosterone, so I really needed to watch what I was eating. I made a promise to her and to myself that I would get my act together. I left her office and drove straight to the Cape, still in shock over the fact that I had gained thirty pounds. It didn't help that as I got out of the car and pulled my bag out of the trunk, my friend Digger walked by on his way to the beach and yelled, "Hey, Chris, you're really puttin' on a few back there."

I already felt like a lard-ass, but now I had verbal confirmation. Thanks, Digger.

What I didn't realize, though, was that Digger was just trying to embrace my new gender and treat me like one of the guys. His wife came by the next day to tell me so. He'd told her what he said to me and she yelled at him. He defended himself by saying that's what guys do: They bust on each other, especially about weight. But when I didn't sling an insult back at him or laugh it off, he worried that maybe I wasn't aware of that particular piece of "guy code" yet. I wasn't, but now that I was, I wanted to make sure he knew we were square. Digger's hairline was receding big time, so when I saw him the next day, I greeted him with "Hey, Dig, you're really goin' bald there." He laughed and punched me in the arm. All square.

I decided then to make some major changes in my eating habits. I cut french fries down to only once a day and eventually to just three times a week. Sometimes I even ate salad. *As a meal.* I allowed myself dessert only on weekends, switched from regular Coke to Diet Coke, and started running four to five days a week. It took me a year to put on the weight and the same amount of time to take it off, but there was still one problem: Unlike what I'd read and was told, the testosterone was not redistributing my body fat in the hip area the way I'd expected it to. The hormones were supposed to flatten out my hips to give me a more masculine appearance, but for some reason that just wasn't happening no matter how much I exercised or worked out. I kept thinking back to Gram's letter and what she said about the hairdresser with the "round butt." *She jinxed me!*

I know, I know, there are lots of guys with round butts and big hips. That's why "dad jeans" were invented. But I was hypersensitive about passing, not to mention a perfectionist. For me, there was only one solution: lipo. And after a month of wearing a girdle-like compression garment under my pants, I had nearly invisible hips and a butt that earned Gram's seal of approval. I was looking more like a guy and, as I'd soon find out, I was acting more like one too.

••

Beth's voice had begun to sound like an unintelligible adult from a Charlie Brown cartoon. A few minutes earlier I'd simply asked if her sister would be joining us for dinner. Ten minutes later I was still waiting for the story she was telling to lead me to the answer. Finally I snapped.

"So is she joining us or not?"

"Hey, I was getting to that. What's wrong with you? You usually like my stories."

"I don't know, it's just . . . I asked you like ten minutes ago. It was a simple question."

"You know, Mandy and I have both noticed you've been a lot more impatient lately *and* less sensitive. We think it's that damn testosterone."

They were right. I had kind of noticed it too, but never made the connection. My tone was different and not just because my voice had changed. I was more confident, sticking up for my ideas and speaking up more in meetings. I was couching things less and being more direct—telling it like it is, both inside and apparently outside the office.

"Oh no. Am I turning into a dick?"

"No, you're not a dick," Beth said. "You're just more like a guy. I just have to get used to it."

So did I. When I began the injections, I was well informed of the physical changes the testosterone would have on my body. But I was not prepared for the emotional ones. While going through this adjustment period, it became clear to me that a lot of male and female gender stereotyping is definitely rooted in legitimate hormonal differences. Take aggression for example. As a woman, I used to watch guys get into drunken arguments that escalated into fistfights and wonder what the hell was wrong with them.

Then, after a few months on testosterone, there I was throwing the first punch. At a Halloween party . . . dressed as a used Kleenex.

I was entertaining a group of my female friends with one of my classic stories. Just as I was getting to the good part, this douche bag dressed in a *Top Gun* flight suit appeared in the doorway, mirrored sunglasses and all. He was jealous I was getting all the girls' attention and made it his mission to knock me down a few pegs.

"Man, you're short," he announced.

I ignored him and went on with my story.

"Seriously, you are *really* short."

One of my friends yelled, "Shut up, asshole," but he wouldn't and began closing the distance between us.

"Doesn't it bother you when you're with a girl and she's taller than you?" he baited.

"Look around. It doesn't seem to bother them."

With that comeback all the girls started cheering, which only pissed him off even more. He came closer, his stocky 5'10" frame towering over me.

"Seriously, I wanna know how tall you are."

"Seriously, why don't you shut the fuck up?"

"Why don't you make me?"

And with that I launched myself at him and if someone hadn't gotten in between us, he would've beaten the snot out of me, which would have been only fitting considering my costume. It was then I realized the quick wit that served me well as a girl could now lead to a major ass-kicking as a guy. I may not have back up next time. In the future I was going to have to check my tongue and my testosterone at the door if I wanted to avoid getting into fistfights.

The point is, most gender stereotypes are based in endocrinology. Men are expected to be more outspoken and aggressive than women. Well, why wouldn't we be, with all that testosterone pumping through our bodies? Women are more sensitive and emotional than men, right? Well, it's a lot easier to be that way when your body is flooded with estrogen—trust me, I know. Take the old adage, *boys don't cry*. Before going on testosterone, I was depressed, so crying was something I did quite often. Like many women, I found it to be an emotional release. A way to "get it all out" and move on. But about a month into the injections, the tears wouldn't come. Even on my saddest days—nothing. I'd think about the worst things, like people I loved dying—still nothing. I even brought out the big guns: *Terms of Endearment*. That scene toward the end when Debra Winger is dying in her hospital bed and saying goodbye to her two boys? I thought for sure that would do it, but nope. Dry as a bone. I was starting to worry I'd never be able to cry again.

I spoke to my doctor and he told me not to worry. He said I might cry less than before but that I certainly hadn't lost the ability. He was right. After I got my tonsils out and the pain meds wore off, oh, there were tears. Later on, when my favorite cousin, Candy, passed away, I cried throughout the entire memorial service and funeral. The year my mom went through chemo? Daily cry-fest. And when my girlfriend broke up with me right before my flight home? T.A.B.—Total Airport Breakdown.

Bottom line: If a guy cries less than a girl, it isn't necessarily because he is unfeeling or less emotional. More likely, it's due to his hormonal make-up. Unless, of course, he really is just a dick.

On the upside, all these negative side effects of testosterone were overshadowed by one major bonus: My periods had stopped. *Free at last, free at last. Thank God Almighty, I was free at last.* The cramps, bloating, lower-back pain, mood swings, risk associated with wearing white pants, and humiliation of having to shop in the feminine protection aisle . . . I was done with that living hell. I threw a "pad-burning party" for my envious female friends and gave away whatever boxes of tampons and bottles of Midol I had left.

After the party, I thought back to that stormy night on the Cape when I first got my period. I knew it was all over for me then. I was male but my body was definitely female, and every month I would get a five-day reminder of the cruel joke God had played on me. Fourteen years later, the joke was finally over and the monthly reminder, gone.

But there were still two other "reminders" that needed getting rid of.

BYE BYE BOOBIES

January 1996

There are a few different techniques surgeons use to perform "top surgery." It really depends on the patient's skin elasticity and chest size. You listen as the doctor explains your options and weigh the pros and cons. This is what my mom and I were doing as we sat in the office of Dr. D, a tall, sturdy woman with a no-nonsense haircut and impressive list of credentials. She came highly recommended by her peers in the plastic surgery field and the guys in my support group. Her warmth and compassion, combined with her extensive medical knowledge and surgical expertise, made us feel like I'd be in very good hands.

Having received letters from my therapist and endocrinologist confirming my transgender diagnosis and their continued involvement in my care, Dr. D had no reservations about performing a bilateral mastectomy on a twenty-six-year-old, perfectly healthy biological female. And after a quick examination of my chest, she told us there were basically two ways I could go.

The first would achieve the best male aesthetic but would require incisions under my pectoral muscles, which would leave me with large, noticeable u-shaped scars. "She—I mean, *he's*—a keloid former," Mom interjected, letting the doctor know that when I heal, my scars tend to be noticeably thicker and larger than average due to the overgrowth of collagen.

The second option was liposuction. Because my boobs were relatively small, the doctor could make tiny half-inch incisions around the areola and under the armpits just wide enough to insert a cannula and suck out the fatty breast tissue. There would be minimal scarring but I would need one or two more touch-up procedures and the shape of my chest would not look as defined as the first option.

Hmmm.

A better-defined male-looking chest was obviously the most desirable outcome. But who was going to notice the definition of my pecs with two thick smiley face scars permanently grinning at them? Then again, I already had some hair on my chest from the testosterone and wondered aloud if over time it would cover the scarring should I choose the first technique. But as Dr. D pointed out, hair can't grow on scar tissue. So if I wanted to hide those scars, I'd likely have to do some creative styling with my chest hair. Doubtful it would ever be long enough to fashion a Donald Trump comb-over, I decided on liposuction. Mom agreed and we set up a surgery date for mid-January. If I had to be out of commission for four to six weeks, it might as well be during the dead of winter.

You'd think someone who was voted Most Likely to Get an Ulcer would be stressing out before going into surgery for the first time. But sitting in the outpatient waiting area with my mom, I was uncharacteristically calm. I was so excited to get rid of these "booby prizes" that I never worried about the process. I had no idea what I was in for and I didn't care. I just wanted them gone.

I was escorted to a tiny room in pre-op where I changed into a pair of geriatric-looking open-toe stretchy socks and a cotton gown that tied in the back but still left my ass hanging out for all to see. Then I lay down on a gurney while a nurse stuck me three times before finally hooking me up to an IV. While I reeled from the sting of that experience, another nurse put what looked to be a shower cap on my head, thereby completing the act of robbing me of my dignity. That's when someone from anesthesia strolled in to make sure I was aware of all the risks involved with the procedure, including that I might die.

Great. At least I'll look hot in my shower cap, open-ass gown, and support hose.

Soon Dr. D showed up in her scrubs to let me know it was time. Mom kissed me goodbye and I was wheeled around a maze of corridors to the OR. A big, bright light shone in my face while masked medical professionals in shades of teal and blue talked nonchalantly about their weekends as though they were in a cafeteria. It was like I wasn't even there. After a few minutes a friendly voice addressed me by name and asked me to count back from a hundred. *99, 98, 97 . . .*

When I woke up, I felt like I'd been run over by an eighteen-wheeler. The kind with naked-lady silhouettes on the mud flaps doing seventy-five in the passing lane. I heard the beeping and chirping sounds of hospital equipment and a woman's voice saying my name over and over again with increasing urgency. I tried to open my eyes, but it felt as though my eyelids were weighted down by sandbags. "Christopher?" (now louder) "Christopher?" (even louder) "Wake up, Christopher!"

Oh my god, will you shut up and let me sleep!

After one more "Christopher," I managed to open my eyes halfway. A nurse in purple scrubs looked back at me.

"You're in recovery," she explained. "The surgery took longer than expected and we're closing."

Closing?

"You need to wake up so we can get you home."

Hospitals close?

"Christopher?"

"I need to throw up."

She handed me a pink plastic basin and I puked my brains out, apparently from the anesthesia. If you're prone to motion sickness like I am, you're more likely to have nausea as a side effect. And the longer you're under, the worse it is. Turns out, like me, Dr. D is a perfectionist: I was under for nine hours instead of the six that were allotted.

Mom came in as the nurse handed me a Styrofoam cup filled with crushed ice and ginger ale. "How do you feel, Shtiny?"

"Like a truck hit me."

I looked down at my chest, which was wrapped tight like a mummy in white gauze bandages and a compression wrap. I felt a weird sensation like something was missing but couldn't feel much of a difference with all the padding and throbbing pain distracting me. Mom and the nurse helped me out of bed and into my clothes. The button-down shirt was definitely a good call; there was no way I'd be able to lift up my arms or pull anything on over my head. It was during this dressing procedure that I noticed the four rubber pouches dangling below my underarms and waist. Shaped like small pears, they were clinging to my body like ticks and filled with varying levels of bloody pulp.

"What are these things?" I asked, fighting off the urge to vomit again.

"Drains," the nurse in purple said, "to help get all the fluid out and make the swelling go down faster. Your mom will be emptying them for you and keeping track of the ccs."

"Bloody Mary, anyone?" a nurse in pink joked, causing me to puke up the ginger ale I'd just managed to get down.

After receiving dirty looks from all three of us, Pinky's smile disappeared and she went back to helping cram me into the wheelchair that would be my official transportation out of the hospital.

Eight days later, I was still stuck with the drains but got the okay from Dr. D to remove the bandages. I don't know which I was excited for more: seeing my new chest or finally getting to take a shower. I remember standing in the middle of my parents' plush bathroom as Mom unvelcroed the binder. I took a deep breath and exhaled.

God, that felt good.

Then came the unwrapping of what seemed to be endless layers of bandages, padding, and gauze. I started to feel off-balance without that familiar weight in front. My mom looked at my chest with tears in her eyes. She hugged me and said that I "finally looked right." I turned to face the mirror. I saw my bruised and uneven but very flat chest in the reflection and got dizzy. Mom saw me swaying and caught me before I could fall. I sat down on the edge of the tub and let the sensation pass.

I looked down: Nothing blocked my view of my feet anymore. Mom said it perfectly; even though my chest didn't look great at this stage, I finally felt "right." I couldn't wait to put on a t-shirt and see how it fit. But first I was going to spend a good twenty minutes in a hot shower. I emerged finally feeling clean, grabbed a bath towel, and instinctively wrapped it around myself under my armpits. Realizing I didn't have to do that anymore, I happily cinched it around my waist like a guy. Two steps later it came undone and fell to the floor, leaving me standing in the hallway naked.

I was going to need to practice this.

••

Of all the gender-confirming surgeries I had over the course of seventeen years, my mastectomy was the most life-changing because it made the most difference in how I looked on the outside and felt on the inside. Not having to bind anymore gave me a feeling of liberation and a major confidence boost. And while testosterone didn't increase my height, this surgery actually did. After several people told me I looked taller (one even accused me of wearing lifts!), I measured myself. Sure enough, I had grown about three-quarters of an inch. This was no medical miracle. In fact, the explanation was quite simple: Before surgery, I hunched all the time to disguise the fact I had boobs. Now that they were gone, I was standing up straight. Nonetheless, I was happy to give Dr. D the credit, and she was even happier to take it.

More importantly, thanks to her handiwork, I could now take my shirt off at the beach or pool just like any other guy. I'd had two more minor procedures, and my chest was looking pretty good. But did it look good enough to go shirtless in front of hundreds of coworkers? I debated while sitting at the poolside bar at Arnold's annual summer outing. This year, in addition to having a flat chest, I was thirty pounds lighter with nearly two years of testosterone injections under my belt and a fresh back wax. I scanned the pool deck to see how all the other guys were handling the ninety-degree heat: fifty-fifty shirts and skins, so there was no pressure. Besides, my going shirtless could never trump the infamous Speedo incident of '95. Still, I wasn't ready.

After a few more drinks and extensive cloud coverage, a group of us creatives decided to blow off the pool and enter the volleyball tournament where somehow, despite the pouring rain and alcohol impairment, we ended up advancing to the finals. Even with major downpours, a large crowd gathered to watch. Trash talk between the teams was out of control, and with bragging rights at stake, the game got serious. Guys began stripping off their rain-soaked t-shirts and the competitive side of me contemplated ditching mine too, as it was impeding my performance.

We were down by two and it was my turn to serve. I looked around. Most of the guys without shirts were on the "full-figured" side. This was definitely not the beach volleyball scene from *Top Gun*. Not even close.

Fuck it.

I pulled my sopping wet t-shirt over my head and flung it aside. If nothing else, it would be a good distraction technique. Whether it was or it wasn't, I don't know, but when I was done serving we were *up* by two. And for me, more memorable than the championship win was the team photo in which I proudly posed shirtless as a man for the very first time.

It was a keeper. A true representation of who I am; who I was meant to be. From that point on, I could no longer bear to look at any past photos of myself as a girl. They represented a person I felt no connection with anymore and reminded me of a painful, inauthentic time in my life when I just couldn't bear to live as I was. It's why you won't find any such "before photos" in this book. Because for those of us who've transitioned, it's not about the pain of who we were then. It's about the joy of who we are now.

PLEASE ALLOW ME TO REINTRODUCE MYSELF

1996–1997

I displayed that volleyball team photo proudly on my desk just below the college diploma bearing my new name and wondered what my sorority sisters would think if they saw it. Oh wait, did I not mention I was in a sorority? Yeah . . . so that happened. I had no intention of joining one when I arrived at Colgate, but I soon discovered that the Greek system was the epicenter of campus social life, mainly because back then there was nothing else to do in the two-and-a-half-square-mile village of Hamilton, New York. (The cultural highlight of my four years was the grand opening of the Grand Union supermarket.) If I wanted to be invited to all the major social events and party it up before D-Day like I'd planned, I had to suck it up. So I chose the sorority with the funnest, most down-to-earth members, and since I was rushing as a sophomore and two of my roommates were already in, I easily went from pledge to member. I can't say I regret it. I got to know lots of great people I might never have met otherwise—like Marianne, a member of my pledge class.

Marianne and I were peripheral friends at Colgate. We lost touch after graduation, but when I started at Arnold, she happened to be working in the PR department and was very kind to me during my transition.

One day she called to tell me that our "sister" Brooke was in town and demanded my presence at dinner. Brooke was a riot. She came from Dallas and was the first person I'd ever heard say "y'all" as part of everyday speech. I'd lost touch with her after graduation too, so before committing to dinner, I asked Marianne if Brooke "knew." She said yes and to meet them at the Blue Cat on Mass Ave.

Brooke looked exactly the same as she did in college: cute with stick-straight dirty-blonde hair cut in a bob just above the shoulders. I, of course, did not look the same. And when I approached the table, she looked right at me, then turned away and kept talking to Marianne, who smiled at me knowingly.

"Is this seat taken?" I asked pointing to the empty chair.

"Ah, yeah," Brooke said, and then I saw the glint of recognition in her eyes. "*Oh my god, CHRIS!*" She jumped up and hugged me. "You look great! I love your tie."

"Thanks, I just came from a client meeting."

"Well, you have some catching up to do."

"I know! I haven't seen you in a while."

"No, I meant with the drinking. I'm already on my second martini."

Brooke and I filled each other in on the last few years while Marianne listened patiently. Dinner ended up being appetizers and drinks and more drinks. And then came the ambush.

"So Chris, Marianne says there's a Colgate Alumni event at a bar right near here . . ."

"The Last Drop," Marianne clarified.

I narrowed my eyes at both of them.

"We thought we'd go check it out," Brooke said.

"Well, have fun!" I said.

Then the tag-team began, each of them taking turns telling me how great I looked, that I should totally go, who cares what other people think, and blah blah blah. I explained this had nothing to do with my transition or my confidence. The reason I refused to go to these local alumni events was because of the group of people who organized and attended them. I had gone to one with Hazel the year after we graduated, and we were both turned off by the same pretentious, judgmental snobs we avoided in college.

"We don't have to stay long. I just wanna see who's there," Brooke begged.

"I just told you who's there."

I don't know if it was the alcohol or Brooke's *"Pleeeeeeease, I came all the way from Texas"* that finally got me, but I reluctantly agreed and the three of us headed off to the Last Drop—one of my favorite spots, thanks to its jukebox and dartboards. It was located on the bottom floor of a brownstone, so the space was extremely narrow. The bar was on the left and on the right was a long ledge just wide enough to rest a drink on. On an average night, people lined both sides, leaving just barely enough room to squeeze through to the restrooms, dartboards, and tables in the back. This particular night was no different, except that almost every person lining the walls was a former classmate, each of whom stopped talking and stared directly at me as I made my way to the bar. The only thing missing was the record skip sound effect. I'm talking blatant, up-and-down, full-on staring. No hello, no nothing.

I wasn't the least bit surprised, but Marianne and Brooke were appalled. "What assholes," Brooke said when we finally made it up to the bar. While Marianne quietly apologized for talking me into coming, Brooke addressed the jerks closest to us.

"What're y'all lookin' at?"

"Let's go," Marianne said. "We don't have to stay."

"Oh, we're stayin'," I said, "and you two are buyin'." I was not about to give this group the satisfaction of driving me out. The Last Drop was *my* turf. I told Marianne and Brooke the only thing that bothered me was that by showing up, I'd given them all something to talk about.

"I'll give them something to talk about," Brooke said, and then kissed me.

Full on the lips.

I don't know who was more stunned: Marianne, our former class-mates, or me. What I did know is I suddenly felt very comfortable at that bar. Brooke's kiss, while clearly a joke between us, gave me street cred;

I was just as much a guy as any of the biological males there. While I'll admit the whole experience rattled me a bit, I was now one hundred percent confident I could walk into any event and face people from my past, whether they accepted me or not. Okay, maybe eighty percent.

••

My newfound confidence would soon be tested at the wedding of one of my former college rugby teammates. Despite what you might picture, the Colgate women's rugby team was not a bunch of big, burly lesbians. The women came in all different shapes, sizes, and degrees of hotness. Some were gay, some were straight, and come to find out, one of us was even a guy! But we all shared in camaraderie and tradition—mainly around drinking. Rugby was a club sport, which meant practices were held only three times a week. Friday's practice was "Pub Practice," which consisted of jogging to the off-campus apartment where a keg was waiting (usually having been picked up and delivered by me in order to get out of the jogging). There we'd practice singing and chugging in preparation for the next morning's game. Our team philosophy was that winning the game was less important than winning the after-party, and our reputation for out-singing and out-chugging our opponents was widely known throughout the Upstate NY/Western MA rugby circuit.

Most players were called either by their last name (e.g., Price, Fedin) or a nickname given to them by an elder member. There were some classics—Shiner, Hippie, Pinko, Crash, Thud, Skippy—and last but not least, Swede, who was the one getting married and reuniting the gang, most of whom would be seeing me for the first time as a guy. And having gone through a mastectomy and almost two years of testosterone injections, the change in my appearance at this wedding, unlike my cousin's, would be a lot more dramatic. It might be awkward at first, but they would accept me. I was sure of it . . . kind of.

I made the two-hour drive alone that Sunday but had planned to meet up with Price and Fedin beforehand to avoid having to walk into the church by myself. Instead, I got lost and missed my window of opportunity. Luckily the testosterone had yet to override the female part of my brain that has no qualms about asking for directions so I made it to the church just in time to see Swede make her grand entrance. As she headed down the aisle, I quietly slipped into the back and scanned the pews for any of my former teammates. No luck. The place was packed and everyone was facing front. The only way I'd be able to ID any of them now would be by the familiar maroon jacket that said "Colgate Rugby" on the back, and I highly doubted any of them would be wearing one of those. Well, maybe Keeler.

I sat in the back row by myself, which made me feel all the more self-conscious until I looked across the aisle and saw a pretty girl smiling at me. It was Thud—or was it Crash? I could never remember who was who, and having not seen either of them in four years only made it more challenging. I smiled back and mouthed, "I got lost." She mouthed back, "We did too." Then Crash (or was it Thud?) leaned in and waved.

Well, the good news was they recognized me. The better news was when we met up at the bar at the reception it was as though we were all back at The Jug, minus the crappy beer and all the pushing and shoving. The fact that I was now a different gender didn't seem to matter to anyone. Some even considered it an advantage to have a dance partner at the ready. According to Siedsma, who in her "ho-bag heels" had at least eight inches on me, our performance to "Dancing Queen" was "epic." Not sure what everyone else thought of it, but it did catch the eye of one particular girl at the wedding. She was just my type: short, cute, and blonde with glasses that screamed, "I'm smart but I also know how to have fun." We danced into the night and I'm truly convinced we could've had a future together, had she not been five years old.

••

Swede's wedding was a success, but I had an even bigger test coming: my ten-year high school reunion. Most reasons people are insecure about attending such an event involve weight gain, hair loss, or lack of impressive career stats—not a gender change. Still, I had a common dilemma:

What to wear? Standing in front of my closet, I cursed myself for letting my four best friends talk me into going. They were all girls and the only Waylandites I still hung out with. Back in 1987 we were known as the "Fab Five"—well, at least that's what we called ourselves. "Mare" (Most Class Spirit) and "Schu" (Kindest Heart) were class president and vice president, so it was their responsibility to plan the reunion and make sure the other three-fifths of us attended. "Meek" (Cutest) and "Mel" (Best Looking) were in from the beginning. Getting me (Most Likely to Get an Ulcer), to go took a lot more convincing. I held out right up until the week before the event when Schu said something during her final plea: "Everybody knows, P-Head. They're going to ask me how you are and probably *where* you are. What do you want me to tell them?"

It was then that I realized no matter how Schu answered that question, everyone was just going to assume I didn't show up because I didn't have the balls. And while that might have literally been true (that surgery was still a few years away), figuratively I had developed quite a set of *cojones*. I was not about to let people think I was ashamed or embarrassed about myself. I was going.

But I was going to get really drunk first.

After settling on gray flannel pants and a black cashmere sweater, I walked over to Schu's North End apartment, where the Fab Five plus one husband and one boyfriend were gathering for pre-party beverages. I entered to cheers, hugs, and a shot glass filled with tequila—the latter of which only made my stomach feel worse.

Meek put her arm around my shoulder. "Are you ready for this, P-Head?"

"I will be after a few more drinks."

On the way to the event I reminded everyone of the four rules:

1. No one was to leave me alone with anyone for the first hour.
2. After that, if I was ever spotted talking to a class member by myself for more than ten minutes, someone had to come in for the save.
3. To avoid any awkward men's room situations, a Fab Five husband or boyfriend was to accompany me whenever I needed to go.
4. I was to have a full vodka soda in my hand at all times.

The reunion took place in the lounge area of Michael's Restaurant and Bar on Commercial Street. It was a big open space that had a pool table in the back and a huge, well-staffed, and well-stocked bar. To get to this section, you had to pass through the restaurant and go up a few steps, which we were all about to do when I heard a voice from a nearby table call my name. I turned to find an Arnold employee getting up from her chair and heading toward me. I turned back and my drunk-ass friends had all moved on to the party without me.

Shit! We'd been there thirty seconds and all of them had already broken rule #1.

After about two minutes of small talk, I informed my coworker that my high school reunion was going on in the next room and I needed to go make an appearance. She looked at me with sympathy, commented on my bravery, and wished me luck. I took a deep breath and headed up the short flight of three stairs. There at the top stood a tall, slim, good-looking guy with a receding hairline and a warm smile.

"Chris?"

"Yessss," I said slowly, buying myself time to determine which former classmate this was.

"Mike," he helped.

"Oh my god, Mike Ball!" I shouted, proud of myself for remembering his last name. He was one of the nicest guys in our class.

"Yes!" he said, and in lieu of the hug he would've given me as "Kris," he appropriately stuck his hand out. I shook it, and relied on my sense of humor to break the ice.

"If anything, I thought people would have trouble recognizing *me*."

Mike laughed and said he'd heard the news a while ago, adding that he was proud of me for both doing what I needed to do to be happy and having the guts to come to the reunion. I asked him for an update on his life, and mid-synopsis, Meek showed up with my vodka soda and joined in the conversation. Rules #1 and #4: check.

I don't think I left that spot for a good hour. Once people got wind I was there they sought me out, girls giving me hugs and saying how great I looked, guys shaking hands and for the most part treating me no differently than they would've before. Throughout the night, I chatted with dozens of classmates I hadn't seen in years. And while my prom date was a no-show, I did run into the guy I had my first kiss with at the eighth-grade dance. He came right up and said hello and how great it was to see me. I wondered if he had mistaken me for somebody else until he used my name when introducing me to his wife.

Honestly, I could not believe how mature everyone was. When mentally preparing myself for this event, I'd made the mistake of thinking my classmates would react to me like high school kids, not twenty-eight-year-old adults with jobs, spouses, and families. This thought was quickly interrupted by, "Hey Chris, I forgot how short you were!"

And I forgot how obnoxious you were.

That said, with the initial meet-and-greets done and the alcohol fully kicked in, I was having a grand old time. I have a hazy recollection of talking the Stanton twins' ears off and shooing Meek away when she innocently tried to enact the save rule. "I'm not going anywhere," I slurred, "I'm talking to Cheryl and Daryl." Little did I know Meek was trying to save *them,* not me.

In the end, my fellow Fab Fivers had to drag me out of there.

The next day, at Sunday dinner, my family was dying to hear how it went.

"It was really fun," I said washing down two Advil with a glass of ice water. "Everybody was really cool about it."

Mom cut to the chase, "Well, what did you say when you walked in?"

"I said, 'You should've voted me Most Likely to Get a Sex Change.'"

BUSINESS OR PLEASURE?

Spring 1996

In the middle of all my social "debuts," I also made my first official dating debut. I was more comfortable in my body than I had ever been and decided it was time to put myself out there. Truth be told, I had some extra motivation: Jess. She was calling a lot more now that her boyfriend and the hardest years of law school were both behind her. She might have lived hundreds of miles away in Chicago, but it felt like we were getting closer. I saw my opening and I took it.

"Soooo . . . hypothetically, if I were to ask you out on an official date, would you say yes?"

Jess laughed, "Ah, that's not really the way to ask someone out on a date, but yes, I would say yes."

My heart jumped. "Okay, well, I'm kinda new at this," *Are we flirting?* "I have to be in Chicago in a couple weeks for focus groups. I thought maybe I could take you to dinner while I'm in town."

"It's a date," she said.

Turns out the hotel where I was staying was just a few blocks from the law office where Jess was clerking, so I gave her my room number and she met me there after work. She looked as beautiful as I remembered and her blue eyes went wide when she saw me. We hugged each other, longer and tighter than what would be considered platonic. As she let go, she said that now it felt "right."

I knew exactly what she meant. I was never comfortable hugging anyone when I had boobs. Even though they weren't that big, they were there like two foreign bodies always in the way and always reminding me I was the wrong gender. I figured I was the only one who noticed it, but I guess Jess had always felt my male energy. And now with my flat chest, that energy matched my physical body. I was just surprised to hear her verbalize it the way she did. I was even more surprised to see she'd brought an overnight bag. She was going to change her clothes for dinner and figured since her office was so close to my hotel it would be easier to just stay over than drive all the way home.

I didn't want to be presumptuous but this was shaping up to be the best first date ever.

We went to an Italian restaurant, drank a bottle of wine, and caught up. I asked her about lawyer stuff and how her family was doing. She asked about my family and kept telling me how great I looked and how much happier I seemed. She too said I looked taller. I told her she didn't have to flatter me if she was trying to get lucky. I was a sure thing.

Now for those of you expecting an E.L. James-esque account of what went on in my room, you will be extremely disappointed. This is not *Fifty Shades of Grey*. The truth is, while I was happy with my body from the waist up, I was nowhere near comfortable with it from the waist down, so our night together was strictly PG, as in "Pretty Great"!

The following months with Jess, however, were rated G, as in "Gone." She made a few trips out to Boston but split her time between me and her sister, who was attending graduate school in Cambridge. I began to notice I always got the short end of the stick. Her calls became less frequent and mine were rarely returned. I tried to tell myself she was just busy. I knew the hours lawyers were expected to bill. I'd read *The Firm*. But it was getting old. And I was tired of feeling hurt.

Then I hit my breaking point.

With two days' notice, Jess called to tell me she was visiting her sister for the weekend and asked if I'd be around. I said yes and that I'd love to see her Saturday. She said she'd call me Friday. I never heard from her. On Sunday morning she called to see if I could meet her for lunch and then drive her to the airport. Even though I was pissed, I agreed. I figured we could at least talk and I could get some things off my chest. When I showed up at the restaurant, I was stunned to see Jess' sister and her boyfriend sitting at the table. I ate my chicken club silently fuming and feeling like I was just being used for a ride to Logan. On the drive there, Jess said the next time she came, she'd carve out more time for me.

"Something tells me there won't be a next time," I said.

She looked surprised. "What do you mean?"

I went off. I told her it was obvious she didn't want to spend any time alone with me and that whatever romantic feelings she'd had for me had clearly changed. I strongly suspected there might be someone else, but kept that to myself—mainly because if there was, it would've killed me. I told her I was tired of being blown off and, without giving her a chance to respond, ended the conversation and whatever was left of our relationship with five words:

"Don't ever call me again."

I said those words partly out of anger and partly because I felt to get over her I needed to take back control. The only way to stop myself from sitting around waiting for her to call was to tell her not to. That way I wouldn't have any expectations. It worked for a while, but those words haunted me. I'm not a mean person. I'd never cut anyone out of my life like that before. Around six months later I had a terrible nightmare that Jess died and I was wracked with guilt for leaving things the way I did. I dialed her work number. Her assistant asked for my name and then put me through. I felt immediate relief when I heard Jess's voice say hello in her normal cheerful manner.

"Jess, it's Chris . . . Edwards."

"I know," she said warmly. "How are you?"

"I'm good. I, I had a bad dream about you and just wanted to make sure you were okay and um . . . not dead."

"I'm fine." I could hear she was smiling.

I told her I'd been feeling really bad about the way I'd left things and that I said what I said because I needed to get over her. She said she understood and we ended the call both feeling better.

Hanging up the phone, a calm washed over me. I can't say I was truly over her, but I was finally able to let go of the fantasy of spending the rest of my life with her. It was time to look forward and open my heart to the possibility of a real, tangible relationship—one that didn't exist in my head. It was something I definitely longed for; I just wasn't sure I was ready to put myself out there again.

Until I met Lucy.

••

You know that saying, "Never fish off the company pier"? Well, it doesn't apply to ad agencies. Arnold, like many other shops, was extremely incestuous. There were indiscreet make-out sessions at Christmas parties, rumors (both confirmed and unconfirmed) of interdepartmental off-site hook-ups, and full-on dating right out in the open. Lucy and I fell into the last category.

Lucy was an "Ass Pro" or assistant producer, and our romance bloomed while on a shoot in Sydney, Australia, in 1998. I was producing major TV spots for a financial services company, one of which was going to air on the Super Bowl. As a senior writer, I was in way over my head. The spots relied heavily on computer-generated imagery (CGI), with which my partner and I had little experience. We were also solely responsible for the print and radio campaigns as well as an internal marketing effort for the company. The fourteen-hour time difference was killing us, we weren't seeing eye to eye with the director, and during a critical juncture in the shoot, the producer we'd come to rely on had to fly home due to a family emergency.

Lucy ended up being my confidant through it all. She was only twenty-three, six years younger than me, but I found her wiser than her years. She had a boyfriend she was lukewarm on, but I still didn't think she was interested in me. I thought maybe she looked up to me as a senior creative or big brother type, but discovered she'd had a crush on me a year earlier when she was an intern. She'd seen me give a presentation and thought I was cute and funny. She had no idea I was transgender until she was officially hired at Arnold. Apparently that piece of knowledge freaked her out a little and caused her to keep her distance, but after four weeks with me in Sydney, she fell victim to my charms.

When word of our relationship spread around the office, people treated both of us differently. Lucy was hot (think Evangeline Lilly as Kate from *Lost*), so I had instant credibility with the guys. Dating Lucy also changed the perception of other girls who, like her, might have initially been freaked out by my gender history. I now had validation on both fronts. It was a win-win.

Lucy's experience, however, was not quite so positive. She was barraged with questions, but not the ones you'd think. They were less about what it was like dating someone who was transgender and more about what it was like dating the CEO's son: *Do you ever have dinner with Ed? Have you been to the Cape house?* Coworkers began excluding her from bitch sessions because they were afraid she now had a direct line through me to the top. I told her not to worry—that I went through the same thing when I first started and it would wear off. I also warned her people might now say things to her on purpose in the hope that it would get to my father. That happened to me a lot.

But working together wasn't why our relationship ended after just eight months. Unfortunately for Lucy, she was my first "real" girlfriend. So while most guys would have had lots of practice by age twenty-nine, I was making high school mistakes. At parties and social events, I was my same outgoing self—talking to everyone, dancing with everyone. I didn't expect I was supposed to adjust my behavior because I now had a girlfriend. I figured that was my personality and what she liked about me. And due to my gender history, I tended to have mostly female friends. Lucy and every woman I've been with since has had trouble with this at some point. They think: *Why does he need to hang out with other girls now that he has me?* You can see how this might cause problems.

Then there was our age difference. Six years isn't that much, but twenty-three and twenty-nine are two very different life stages. I figured Lucy was so young she wouldn't be looking for a serious relationship, which was perfect for me because I was just starting to date. I was wrong. She *was* looking for long-term commitment, and I couldn't give it to her. Nor could I give her the intimacy she needed. I had declared my body from the waist down off limits, which made "sexy time" very one-sided. I figured no woman would complain about that—all the more focus on her—but I learned from Lucy there needs to be mutual give-and-take for a physical connection to be an emotional one. Someone more experienced probably would've gotten that.

Looking back though, the defining factor was the L-word. I remember the exact moment when Lucy told me she loved me. We were in my car. I was dropping her off at home and out of the blue she blurted it out. I froze.

"You don't have to say it back," she said. "I just thought you should know." Then she smiled and got out of the car, closing the door behind her. I waited to make sure she got in okay and knew I was in trouble when she walked right into the house without turning around and waving to me like she usually did.

"I'm an asshole," I thought as I drove off.

The fact was I did love her, but I was operating under the fucked-up notion that you weren't supposed to tell a person that unless you knew he or she was "The One." Someone with more dating experience probably would've known that too.

Lucy tried her best to pretend like my silence didn't bother her, but it did. We broke up soon after. It was then that I told her I loved her but hadn't said it because I wasn't sure I wanted to marry her. She looked at me like I was crazy and informed me that she wasn't sure she wanted to marry me either. So naturally we got back together. Only to officially call it quits a month later.

I knew it was the right thing but I still felt sad and empty afterward, fearing there would never be another girl as open-minded as Lucy who would accept me and my "transgenderness." It was the one thing about my transition that I couldn't control.

TAKE MY UTERUS. PLEASE.

January 1997

I was wearing jeans and a navy cashmere sweater when I caught her staring at me. She was cute—blonde, mid twenties, funky glasses. She returned my smile with a disdainful glare and went back to reading her magazine. I guess I shouldn't be surprised, seeing that I was a guy sitting by myself in the waiting room of the Women's Health Center for Excellence. I felt more out of place than I did in my pediatrician's waiting room. At least there I wasn't on the receiving end of sisterhood animosity.

Many transgender men view the hysterectomy step as unnecessary—the testosterone has already stopped the periods from coming so why bother? It's just more invasive surgery and a lot more money to pony up, as insurance likely won't cover it without a documented cancer diagnosis. And once it's all over, it's not like you can physically tell or feel any difference.

I can't speak for anyone else's choices, but I can tell you why I felt so strongly about having the procedure: I wanted everything feminine about me *gone*.

Even something as seemingly minor as the tiny holes in my ear lobes. While they had partially closed up, you could still tell they had been pierced, and I became very self-conscious about it during my transition phase with my sideburns and shorter haircut.

I'd overheard my editor telling a client about how her earlobe had torn from wearing heavy, dangly earrings so much. She said she found a great plastic surgeon just a few blocks away who stitched it right up. It was quick and painless and didn't leave a scar. I mentioned this to my parents who talked me out of it, saying I was crazy—that no one could even tell my ears were pierced to begin with. Then one day at lunch I caught Babs staring at me with a quizzical look on her face.

"Shtiny, do you have pierced ears?"

That's it. I'm making an appointment.

The next week I found myself face-to-face with my editor's plastic surgeon, ready for the twenty-minute procedure. He said he would be using extremely fine stitches on the inside and that the most anyone would ever see (if they were up real close) would be the tiniest vertical hairline scar and even that would fade away over time. What he failed to mention, however, was that I'd be walking out of his office looking like Frankenstein, which is what a friend of mine called me when she spotted me on my way home. She saw the zigzagging navy blue thread used on the "surprise" exterior stitches and asked what the hell happened. I told her I had cysts removed, which is what I continued to say for the next week until the stitches came out. Funny, I had no trouble telling people I was having my uterus removed but needed to make up a story about getting rid of ear-piercing holes. Maybe it was because they were visible to everyone and my uterus wasn't.

Regardless, just knowing my reproductive organs were there made me uncomfortable. I didn't want to have to see a gynecologist for pelvic exams and pap smears and worry about getting ovarian, uterine, or cervical cancer down the road. Those were women's issues and I wanted nothing to do with them. I wasn't sure I wanted children, and even if I did, as a man I wasn't about to get pregnant and give birth even if I had the capacity to do it. As far as I was concerned, all those "female parts" inside me had the potential to do more harm than good both physically and emotionally. My parents eventually understood and once again Mom said she'd take care of me and Dad said he'd take care of the bills. It was not lost on me how lucky I was. Still, luck wasn't doing anything to shield me from the suspicious looks I was getting from the other women in the waiting room and I eagerly gave up my seat for a private one inside the surgical gynecologist's office.

My surgeon came highly recommended by Dr. D, who had, to my relief, already filled her in on my special circumstance. She had a professional, buttoned-up demeanor and an extra-firm handshake. There was no small talk or joking around. She launched right into all the procedural options, outlining the difference between a hysterectomy (uterus) and total hysterectomy (uterus and the cervix) and then asked me if I wanted to keep my ovaries. I had assumed they were part of the whole reproductive apparatus and would be removed along with everything else. She said most people think that too but that it's actually a separate procedure. She asked if I wanted to have children or harvest any eggs to be frozen for future use. I passed on both options. If I ever did decide to do the kid thing, I wanted it to come from my wife's eggs. When the doctor asked me what I'd do if my future wife turned out to be infertile, I told her I'd cross that bridge when I came to it. At this point in my life I had no girlfriend and no interest in having kids; the last thing I wanted was to be responsible for another person. I'd been living the last twenty-seven years of my life for other people. I finally just wanted to focus on myself.

We mapped out my surgery, deciding on a total hysterectomy and salpingo-oophorectomy, which would remove all female reproductive organs and eliminate any future need for gynecological exams. She told me the surgery would take an hour or so and that I might not need to stay overnight. I'd have a horizontal scar across my lower abdomen resembling that of a C-section (today the procedure can be done laproscopically with very little scarring), and the recovery time would be about four weeks. I set the date for January 1997 and looked forward to starting the New Year uterus-free.

••

When I woke up, I didn't feel nearly as bad as I did after my mastectomy. I wasn't even nauseated, which was a huge relief. I felt a hand squeeze my arm.

"Hi, Shtiny."

My mom was there—an even bigger relief. I tried to sit up but my abdomen wasn't havin' it. I surveyed my surroundings. It looked nothing like the curtained-off section I had in recovery at the last hospital. I had my own private room! I was amped until Mom informed me that yes, it was a private room, but no, I was not in recovery. I was here for the night—possibly two.

What? I asked her if something went wrong with the surgery.

"No," she said. "It didn't even take an hour."

So what was the big deal? I had endured a nine-hour bilateral mastectomy and went home that same evening. This surgery took under an hour and relatively speaking, for someone who'd just had his insides scooped out, I felt pretty good. My mom agreed that it was ridiculous but my doctor went "by the book" and most patients after a hysterectomy are in the hospital for two to three days.

When Dr. By-the-Book came to check on me, she was all smiles. She said my surgery couldn't have gone better and that it was the fastest hysterectomy/salpingo-oophorectomy she'd ever performed. Apparently sixteen months of testosterone injections had shrunk my entire reproductive system to the size of a fifty-cent piece, making it extremely easy to remove. (Why I was left with a twelve-inch scar is still beyond me.)

"So why can't I go home?" I asked. Mom even made a plea as a nurse, hoping that might sway her. Nope.

"I want you here overnight," she said. "Two nights is protocol but since you're young and healthy, I'll let you go home tomorrow if all goes well."

Fine. How bad could one night be? Doped up on pain meds, I figured I'd sleep right through. Ha. Was I in for a rude awakening—in more ways than one! My room was right outside the nurses' station. So between their voices, the constant beeping of hospital equipment, and beleaguered cries from patients in desperate need of ice chips, I would've had better luck trying to sleep through a prison riot. Not to mention every time I did manage to doze off I was awakened by a medical student checking my vital signs (yes, I'm still alive!) or worse, attempting to draw blood.

When my doctor showed up at 8:00 a.m., I was practically homicidal. She flipped through my chart and told me everything looked great. A few hours later, she finally let me go home. And while I was psyched to put that hospital stay in my rearview, I knew it was only the beginning.

"BOTTOM SURGERY"

Spring 1998

It's a lot easier to turn a penis into a vagina than a vagina into a penis. Which might explain why more transgender women choose to undergo surgery: One or two operations can yield very good results and run maybe $25,000 or less. Building a penis is a lot more complex and way more costly. As many doctors and my mom have put it, it's a lot harder to add than it is to subtract.

Phalloplasty, as it is called, requires multiple procedures with lengthy recovery times and the potential for numerous complications. Add a six-figure price tag for what I like to call the "deluxe model," and it's no wonder "bottom surgery" is not as popular with transgender men. Some choose to stop after the mastectomy and forgo it altogether. Others pass on phalloplasty and opt instead for a less complicated, less expensive surgery called metoidioplasty. This involves taking the clitoris, which has been slightly enlarged due to testosterone, and releasing or untethering it so it hangs like a penis. If size matters, this is probably not the surgery for you.

I knew I wanted bottom surgery and, based solely on the medical literature I'd dug up, a metoidioplasty wasn't going to cut it for me. I was born both a Taurus and a perfectionist, which meant I was willing to go through whatever it would take to get myself the closest thing to a fully functioning biological penis. I wanted to pee standing up. I wanted to be able to have intercourse—to feel what it's like to be inside a woman. I wanted all those things that most genetic men take for granted because they were born with what I lacked.

What I didn't know was that finding the right doctor would be so difficult. When I began my search back in late 1996, there were only a handful of surgeons that performed phalloplasties in the United States and Canada. The Internet was relatively new so there was very little research one could do online. I relied on information from gender clinics, Bet's knowledge, word of mouth from my support group, and eventually consultations with the doctors themselves. The most well-known surgeon in the field at the time was Dr. Donald Laub. Based out of Stanford in Palo Alto, California, he was a pioneer in gender reassignment surgery, inventing and evolving procedures since the 1970s. There was a doctor on the East Coast who was newer to the field and was adopting Dr. Laub's technique, but when I mentioned him to my support group, I heard only bad reviews. Two of the guys told me they'd gone to his clinic for consultations and were treated more like dollar signs than people. Another member said he'd also heard that from someone else. A fourth guy said he knew someone personally who'd had his surgery done by this doctor and was now seeing Dr. Laub to try to "fix it."

Yikes!

They all said if I was going for the deluxe model, Laub was the best choice. I asked them about the Canadian surgeon I'd read about and received a resounding STAY AWAY.

I saw Bet that week and told her of my progress. She said she'd heard good things about Dr. Laub too and also told me about a surgeon in Florida who was doing similar work. Since Florida was a lot closer than California, I decided to go there first, and my mom was happy to join me.

We were at thirty thousand feet en route to the Sunshine State, and I was compiling a list of questions for the doctor.

"Ask him how many penises he's made," Mom said. "And tell him you want to see pictures." Our conversation had become so matter-of-fact that she seemed to have forgotten what the subject matter was. And that we were surrounded by a plane full of people.

"A little louder, Mom. I don't think the pilot heard you."

"Lemme see what you have," she said, reaching for my notepad.

"Okay, hold on a sec." I looked over my list:

- How many phalloplasties have you done?
- How many with microsurgery?
- Can I see pictures? Talk to one of your patients?
- How big will my penis be?
- Do you create the balls—testicles—at the same time?
- How many surgeries will it take to complete?
- Does insurance cover any of them?
- What are the risks?
- What's the recovery time like?
- How will I achieve an erection?
- Will I be able to have an orgasm?

I almost didn't write that last one down. I mean it's not really something you want to ask in front of your mother. But doctors tend to rush you out and I was afraid I'd forget to ask if I didn't have it on paper in front of me.

Before I got to ask the doctor any questions, I had to answer my share. The form I was given to fill out in the waiting room was extensive, but nothing like the phonebook-size packet I was still working on for my upcoming appointment with Dr. Laub.

Once the forms were completed, we were led to a nondescript examination room that was in keeping with the vibe of the rest of the office: very clinical with no personality whatsoever. Within a few minutes I discovered the same could be said for the doctor. He was in his late forties, with a husky build and an arrogance that easily overshadowed it. Worse, there was no compassion. He never smiled, and spoke to me about the surgery as if he were a contractor talking to me about my kitchen renovation: "It'll be a nuisance, but if you want it done, you're just gonna have to suffer through it."

Also disturbing, I couldn't get a straight answer from him on how many phalloplasties he'd performed (somewhere between nine and twenty), and he seemed insulted by the fact that I was asking questions. He was reluctant to show me photos but eventually broke out an album of before and after shots. I was horrified by most of them—even what he deemed to be the "good penises." I knew the surgery was far from perfected, but these penises didn't seem to have much shape to them, let alone well-defined heads. They looked like long blobs and most of them were way too big. I asked if you could pee through them and he said no.

That's when Mom started asking questions and we discovered that he had only a handful of "deluxe model" surgeries under his belt.

"That procedure requires a skin graft to extend the urethra to enable you to pee standing up," he warned. "I'd need to remove all the skin from your inner forearm."

I gulped, "What kind of scar would that leave me with?"

He said flatly, "You'll want to wear long sleeves."

I asked to see photos of a forearm after surgery. He showed us a picture of one that looked like it had been severely burned in a fire from the wrist to the elbow. I turned to my mom, whose jaw had dropped, and turned back to the doctor.

"*That's* what my arm will look like for the rest of my life?"

His response was almost as disturbing as the photo: "Do you want a penis or not?"

That sealed my decision. This dick would not be making my dick. It might be one thing if he created the best penises in the world, but even then I wasn't so sure. This wasn't a "one and done" procedure like my hysterectomy. I'd be in for several surgeries over a period of two years or more. I needed a doctor that I could feel comfortable with. And he wasn't it.

On the way back to the airport Mom tried to make excuses for his horrible bedside manner. Having been an OR nurse, she told me a lot of doctors, especially the skilled ones, are arrogant. I looked at her with my trademark raised eyebrow and she relented. "You're right, Shtine, he was a prick."

With Florida out, we pinned our hopes on Dr. Laub, and soon Mom, Jill, and I were boarding a plane to San Francisco. Since none of us had ever been there before, we decided to turn this surgical consult into a mini family vacation. As Jill and Mom compared advice from Fodor and Frommer, I tried to take my mind off all the "what ifs" in my head: *What if Dr. Laub was also arrogant and insensitive? What if his album of penises didn't look any better? What if he also told me my forearm would look like a burn victim? Then what would I do?*

My fears stayed with me throughout the afternoon as we explored San Francisco. Riding the glass elevator up to our hotel room, I couldn't tell if the anxiety I had was from looking down 150 feet or looking ahead to my meeting with Dr. Laub. I went over my list of questions one more time before bed and tested out the microcassette recorder I had bought for the occasion. There was going be a lot of information to take in, and his coordinator would only allow us half an hour. I argued for more time, reminding her that I was flying across the country just to meet with him, but she wouldn't budge. I'd had three conversations with her, and so far I was not a fan.

The next day as we approached the clinic in Palo Alto, a calm washed over me. Situated in a beautifully landscaped courtyard surrounded by all kinds of plants, flowers, and benches, it was the exact opposite of the utilitarian office building in Florida. The medical suite looked like a California bungalow—stucco with terra-cotta shingles. A woman whose voice I recognized from my previous phone calls greeted us in the court-yard. She was friendly but all business, and after a quick tour of the grounds, escorted us inside.

While we waited, I examined all the framed awards and photos of Dr. Donald Laub covering the walls. He was smiling in every shot and looked like a warm, kind-hearted man. In some of the photos, he posed with children from around the world who suffered from cleft lip and palate deformities. Turns out Dr. Laub had made it his mission to travel

to underdeveloped countries and provide life-changing plastic surgeries
to tens of thousands of people in need, free of charge.

I was blown away. Here I was thinking he just made penises and
vaginas for a living. This man wasn't just a brilliant surgeon; he was a
saint. A humanitarian. I had a good feeling about him and breathed a
sigh of relief as we headed to his office, which felt more like a cozy in-
home library.

Behind an elegant yet unassuming desk sat the pioneer of gender
reassignment surgery, surprisingly in light blue scrubs. His hair was
tousled as though he had just pulled off the matching surgical cap
and rushed over from the OR, knowing he was late for our appointment. He looked to be in his early sixties, and when he stood up to
greet us with a handshake and warm smile, his eyes actually twinkled.
I remember thinking that with a fake white beard and padded red
suit he'd make a great Santa. He motioned for us to have a seat on
the other side of his desk and immediately acknowledged our cross-
country journey as though he were humbled by it. I liked him right
away and knew I'd feel comfortable asking him all the questions on
my list. Anxious to get down to business, I pulled out my cassette
recorder and asked if he minded if I taped our session, telling him I
knew we only had a half hour and I wanted to make sure I didn't forget
anything. He said he didn't mind and that I could certainly have more
of his time if I needed it.

We spent more than an hour together discussing the options for
surgery. We flipped through photos of penises Dr. Laub had created and
noted some were definitely better looking than others. He said when
it came to the quality of results, a lot depended on patient factors like
what their skin was like, if they followed instructions for after-care, and
if they smoked or were overweight. Most of the penises I saw were not
deluxe models, and Dr. Laub did not shrink from that fact. He said that
procedure was still relatively new—not to mention extremely complex
and very expensive—so very few patients opted to go that far. I told
him that I planned to, and asked about the skin graft from the forearm.
He told me his method would not leave me looking like a burn victim;

instead of just taking the skin as is, he would insert a tissue expander into my forearm and gradually fill it with fluid until my arm expanded enough to provide the amount of skin needed to create the urethral extension. He likened the process to how the skin stretches during pregnancy. While I'd have a noticeable scar up my arm from the sutures, it would be nowhere near as frightening as what I saw in the Florida doctor's photo book of horrors.

Dr. Laub cautioned that there are often complications with urethroplasties, mainly infections due to blockages most often caused by hair growth. Apparently when a skin graft is extracted, the hair follicles go with it and hair continues to grow. He took out a red Sharpie and drew an outline on my inner forearm, showing me the large area where I'd need to have six months to a year of electrolysis before he would consider performing the surgery.

My Armo heritage screws me again!

Before I even had a moment to let that sink in, he added that if I wanted balls, tissue expanders would also need to be inserted into my labia and expanded until they were large enough to hold silicone testicular implants. The thought of that made me want to faint, so I moved on to the erection question. Dr. Laub said there were two types of permanent implants: a rigid but bendable rod or a pump device that could be inflated on demand. He quickly added that there is a high risk of these implants eroding through the skin due to lack of sensation down there. This is why patients often choose to forego implants and use a removable rod that can be inserted into the penis just prior to intercourse.

I was beginning to understand why so few people opt for this surgery, and Dr. Laub must have seen it on my face. He had accurately judged me as a perfectionist and wanted to manage my expectations. He quickly emphasized that while the surgery was not perfect, his surgical team was making advances with each procedure and there might be new techniques developed by the time I was ready. He said I was a good candidate but that I should take some time to process everything we discussed. It was a lot to think about for sure. I truly felt like I was going to hurl.

He looked at me and smiled. "Chris, there are people out there who need surgery to stay alive. You're coming out here to get a penis. You're lucky. Remember that."

I wasn't feeling very lucky. But I did get his point.

On the ride back to the hotel, Mom and I agreed on two things:

1. The amount and nature of the surgery I'd have to go through was frightening.

2. Dr. Laub was the man for the job.

She asked me if I was sure I wanted to go through with it. As terrified as I was of the pain, potential complications, and unknown aesthetics, the answer was still, without hesitation, "Yes."

THE ART (AND PAIN) OF HAIR REMOVAL

May 1998

"You'll love her, Eddie," Straubs promised me, "She's so sweet and she's really good and *fast.*"

My friend "Straubs" was setting me up. With her electrologist.

Her name was Deborah and according to Straubs she was both happy and eager to help me. So off I went to Newbury Electrology. As I tried to get comfortable on a lumpy vintage chaise, the young woman seated on the opposite side of the waiting room stole a glance at me and quickly buried her face back in her magazine. *Trust me. It's way more embarrassing for me to be here than you.* To pass the time, I began hypothesizing what she was having done. She didn't seem that hairy but I didn't get a good look at her face. Upper lip maybe? Was a mustache the reason she was hiding behind that outdated *People?* Then it occurred to me if I was imagining what she was doing here, she was probably wondering the same thing about me. Ha! Good luck with that one.

After a few minutes the door to the adjoining room opened and Deborah appeared wearing a white lab coat. She was around 5'1" with fair skin and short dark hair tucked behind her ears. The young woman dropped the magazine she was fake-reading and bolted inside. Deborah turned to me and with a warm smile said, "I'll be right with you, Chris."

Straubs was right. I loved Deborah. She was professional but caring and compassionate. She listened intently as I explained the gravity of my particular hair removal; that it wasn't just for aesthetics. That the skin she would be treating would be used to form the extension to my urethra and if any hair grew inside it, it could cause blockages and infections. She asked a few questions only as they pertained to her job and I answered them, giving her a bit more information than necessary because (1) I could tell she was curious and didn't want to overstep her bounds and (2) as far as I was concerned, Deborah was now part of "Team Edwards," so I wanted her to have all the information she'd need to help my transformation be successful. Plus I just tend to over-share.

I rolled up my sleeve and showed her the seven-inch by three-inch area on the underside of my forearm that I'd marked off. She explained the cycle of hair growth and how over time electrolysis works to permanently destroy the follicles' ability to grow hair. To get the results I needed she suggested thirty- to sixty-minute sessions two to three times a week.

Shit. At eighty bucks an hour, this was gonna add up.

Deborah showed me the machine and the needle she'd be using and then discussed the current strength she felt would be most effective. The trick is finding the balance between pain and efficacy; you want the current strong enough so that the hair can easily be removed with one zap but not so strong that the pain is unbearable. She quickly zeroed in on the right setting, but it was still pretty painful. The machine also made a clicking sound with each zap, which I found unnerving. I began to count the clicks in my head—most thirty-minute sessions getting into the hundreds—and then I'd lose track. Deborah was fast. Zap zap zap, pluck pluck pluck. She covered a lot of ground. After every session, my arm was covered with raised red dots. I wore long sleeves quite a bit that summer.

After nine months of regular treatments, I noticed the hair was growing in thinner and a bit sparser but hadn't disappeared. I took some digital photos of my progress and emailed them to Dr. Laub. He instructed me to keep going and send him more photos in six months. *Six months? I was hoping to have already recovered from my first surgery by then*. I broke the news to Deborah at my next appointment. She gave me a big hug, reminded me that these things take time, and that it was better to be extra diligent with the hair removal now than to go forward with surgery and risk complications. I knew she was right but I was bummed and worried that even after six months, the hair still might not be gone. *Then what?* As if reading my mind, Deborah asked me if I'd ever heard of laser hair removal.

Laser was relatively new in the late '90s and it was pricey. You had to buy a package because it would take three to ten sessions before you'd see a significant reduction in hair growth. It worked best on fair-skinned people with very dark hair. I had the dark hair but olive skin. *Screwed again!* Nonetheless, Deborah reached out to her friend Paula, who had just started performing laser treatments, and told her about my case. She said I should come by to meet with the doctor and he would determine whether or not I was a good candidate.

After confirming with Dr. Laub that this type of hair removal was a legit alternative, I headed to Winchester Electrology and Laser Center and introduced myself to Paula, who was one of the sweetest people on earth. I showed her my forearm and was relieved to hear laser had worked on clients with skin as dark as mine. We chatted for a bit and I immediately felt at ease—a feeling that vanished as soon as the doctor walked in. There was something about him that just seemed "off." He was tall and slim and had very pale, clammy skin. His face looked almost rubbery, which after further examination I attributed to a complete lack of facial hair—no evidence of any beard growth whatsoever. *Odd.* I caught a glimpse of his forearm, which was also completely hairless, and began to wonder if he was his own best customer.

During my five-minute consultation, Dr. Sharpe told me he got his medical degree from Harvard, that despite my olive skin I'd definitely get a good result from the laser, and that I could also benefit from a little lipo on my love handles.

Thanks a lot.

He signed some paperwork, relayed some cryptic instructions to Paula, and then disappeared into his office.

"Do you want to have a treatment now?" Paula asked.

"Do you do it or does he?"

"I do."

"Is he gonna be here every time I come in?"

She looked at me curiously. "No, he's not usually here unless it's for a new patient consult. He dictates the laser setting and I pretty much take it from there. Why?"

"He gives me the creeps. Has anyone else ever said that?"

"No . . . You're the first."

Hmmmm.

Creepy doctors aside, if anyone ever tells you laser hair removal doesn't hurt, I hereby give you permission to punch them in the nose. You may also hear, "Oh, it's not that bad. It just feels like a rubber band snapping on your skin." That one deserves an atomic wedgie. I'd say the sensation is more like being stung by a giant bee. Over and over and over again. And if you think that hurts, try forking over a thousand dollars up front for ten treatments, only to see hair still sprouting. I couldn't understand it. I was coming in every four weeks as directed. Paula even cranked up the setting a bit higher, to my dismay. Were my super Armo hair follicles impervious to laser? The hair had become thinner, but was nowhere near gone.

After further research, Paula found some colleagues who had a brand new type of laser that was said to be stronger and more effective on darker skin. Enter Faye and Margaret, my new best friends. Faye, the older and more experienced of the two, was a riot. Classic Irish: fiery red hair, blue eyes, fair skin, and freckles, with a loud Boston accent that could've landed her a walk-on role in *The Town* (I sway-ah!). Margaret had short dark hair, quiet, compassionate eyes, and skin like porcelain. I pegged her as the more professional and organized one—a good balance to her boisterous counterpart.

Faye examined my forearm and told me that her new laser should work better on the hairs because of some advanced light wave technology thing I didn't understand. And because it emitted a cooling gel after each pulse, she also said it would hurt less. (Not!) But she was right about the first part: This laser did yield better results.

Four or five treatments later, I got home from work and plopped down on the couch with a bowl of cereal and my remote. I flipped on the news just in time to catch the breaking top story about a wealthy, Harvard-educated dermatologist who was arrested for murdering his ex-wife in her home right in front of their daughter. I almost choked on a Mini Wheat when I saw the familiar rubbery face of the man on screen: Just as I thought *No, it couldn't be,* the name "Dr. Richard Sharpe" appeared beneath his image. The story quickly evolved as multiple photos of Dr. Sharpe dressed as a woman surfaced and became the focus of all subsequent news reports. The media thrived on it. He was no longer a murderer. He was a "cross-dressing murderer" or a "transsexual murderer." Nobody really cared about distinguishing the difference between the two because the net takeaway was the same: just like in the movies, man who wants to be a woman equals whack job.

And despite all I'd done to change perceptions, I couldn't help but fear people would apply that same logic to me.

UNDER PRESSURE

Spring 1999

You know ad agency life is a bit fucked up when you need a psychologist on staff. Arnold hired "Dr. Susan" to help upper management in creative and account service "get along." All of us underlings found this amusing. We would see her coming in and out of our bosses' offices and give each other the raised eyebrow. Then one day while I was typing up copy, Dr. Susan appeared in my office. I was completely caught off guard and pretty sure she could tell. To break the ice, she asked me what I was working on.

"An ad for MonsterTrak," I replied. "It's a division of Monster.com, only for entry-level jobs and internships. This ad is supposed to run in *Glamour* magazine. The headline is 'We'll help get your foot in the door—but not in those shoes, girlfriend!'"

She laughed. "That's a good one. I like that."

I smiled. *What is she doing here?*

"Well, I won't keep you, Chris. I just wanted to stop by and introduce myself. Your father told me what your mom was going through and I just wanted to check on you and see how you were doing. Chemotherapy can take quite a toll on everyone."

Three years earlier, we found out Mom had leukemia. My sisters and I didn't grasp the severity of the situation at first because when my parents told us, they played it down so we wouldn't worry. They said "it was the best kind of leukemia to have" and that it was totally treatable with a drug that Mom needed to take in cycles. Well, the doctors were able to treat it for a while, but now she was at the point where she needed a stem cell transplant. We were devastated. In preparation, Mom had to go through some serious chemo and Jill and I were taking turns accompanying her to Dana Farber. "I'm fine," she'd insist. "You don't have to stay. I'll call you when I need to be picked up." She was always strong for us so I tried to be strong for her. But Dr. Susan was right. The stress took a toll on me. Not one day went by when I didn't worry about Mom dying. Add work pressure and my transition hurdles and it's no wonder I'd lost ten pounds and hadn't even noticed.

"It's been hard," I said.

"Why don't I stop by and chat with you for a bit." She opened up her date book and penciled me in.

My partner, Mike, showed up in my doorway just as she was leaving. "Are they afraid you're gonna go postal and shoot up the place?"

"Ha. Ha."

Mentally speaking, I had been doing well with my transition, so my visits to Bet were now prescribed "as needed." I hadn't had a therapy session with her in about a year and a half, so I was out of practice and dreaded delving deep into my psyche again. But Dr. Susan had a totally different style. She was more like a coach than a therapist. There were no stare-down matches or answering questions with more questions. She'd size up a situation, look at it from all angles, and then help me decide on the best path. After some initial hesitation, I looked forward to our visits and no longer cared if anyone saw her coming in or out of my office. They should be so lucky to have her free counsel. Dr. Susan became a valued member of Team Edwards—always there whenever I needed medical guidance or advice with career, relationships, and family.

And she couldn't have showed up at a better time. Because surgically speaking, mine was running out and panic was setting in. I'd received a call from Dr. Laub's coordinator, who dropped a major bomb on me.

"I have some bad news," she said flatly. "Dr. Laub is retiring."

My heart sank. "Wh-when?"

"Next year . . . but he's not taking on any new patients."

"Well, I'm not a new patient. He's already met with me."

"But he hasn't started your surgery yet so technically you're a new patient."

Her matter-of-fact delivery was infuriating.

"Well, I'd like to make an appointment and talk to him myself."

We argued back and forth until she finally gave in and scheduled me another one of her "half-hour specials" for the following month. I hung up the phone victorious but distraught. If Dr. Laub didn't do my surgery, I had nowhere else to turn. I called my mom in tears and recounted the conversation I'd just had. She was furious.

"That bitch!"

"I know, Mom. But she can't help it that he's retiring."

"She can help her attitude! She didn't even ask him. We'll go back and meet with Dr. Laub. He won't say no to you."

After a family strategy session, we decided that Dad would accompany me instead. He had orchestrated many successful business deals and was a master at the art of problem-solving and negotiation. He'd be the best person to have in the room should Dr. Laub say no, and we needed to mediate an alternate solution to my predicament. I think Dad was also hoping to appeal to him father to father.

We arrived at the clinic in Palo Alto, and within minutes were seated in Dr. Laub's office. He immediately focused on my arm and noting all the electrolysis scabs, asked if I'd had a treatment recently. "You have no idea," I said. He told me I should wait a month for the hair to grow and then send him another picture so he could make an accurate assessment. Dad and I looked at each other.

"Does this mean you'll do my surgery?" I asked.

"Why wouldn't I?"

"Well, your coordinator told us you're retiring and that you weren't taking on any new gender patients."

"Well, you're not new. We already had a deal." He smiled, with a twinkle in his eye as though conspiring against "the establishment."

Dad stood up to shake his hand, thanking him profusely. I went around his desk and gave him a hug.

"Let's not keep the doctor any longer, Chris," Dad said, opening the office door and practically shoving me through it. As we darted past reception, the coordinator spotted us.

"Done so soon?"

"Yes, Dr. Laub wants me to send him a picture of my arm in a month and then set up a surgery date."

She looked pissed.

"I'll call you in a month," I shouted as Dad ushered me out the front door.

We were both giddy as we got into the car.

"Sorry to rush you out," Dad said, "but the first rule of business: When you get the answer you want, don't give 'em time to change their mind."

But time would prove to be my enemy once again. One month turned into three months and three months turned into six. After four years of electrolysis and laser treatments, enough of my stubborn Armo hair kept coming back to prevent me from setting a surgery date. I had originally planned to be done with bottom surgery by the year 2000, and here we were in 2002 and I hadn't even started. With Dr. Laub's retirement now closer to reality, my penis was slipping further and further away from it.

Mom tried to make me feel better by telling me maybe this was a sign I wasn't meant to have surgery yet. That maybe there was some surgical breakthrough coming that would be worth the wait. I clung to this hope and tried to stay positive. But the truth was I no longer had control over the timetable of my transition; I had no idea when I'd finally feel complete.

Then something Dr. Susan had said about regaining control popped into my brain: *Knowledge is power. Always get as much information as you can.*

The phone rang three times before Dr. Laub's coordinator picked up.

I swallowed my pride and with desperation in my voice, explained my situation and asked for her advice. In a sympathetic tone uncharacteristic of any of our prior conversations, she told me I couldn't pin my hopes on Dr. Laub. He was retiring because he had brain cancer.

I was stunned. Speechless. How could God let this happen to such a brilliant, compassionate man? The world needed him. *I* needed him. It was then that I realized the reason this woman had been so protective of Dr. Laub's schedule was because she was concerned for his health. I felt a new sense of understanding and appreciation for her. Knowing his condition, I probably would've acted the same way toward any patient that was trying to keep him working.

I began to process what this meant for Dr. Laub, his practice, and the future of gender reassignment surgery and asked if there was anyone at Stanford who could carry on his legacy. She mentioned a few doctors whose expertise was male-to-female, but because female to-male procedures were still far from perfected, she didn't feel there was anyone there I could see at this time.

My heart sank . . . until I heard an enthusiastic "Wait a minute!" on the other end of the line.

WHAT'S UP, DOC?

April 11, 2002

Turns out a young hotshot plastic surgeon who'd trained under Dr. Laub had left Stanford to join a private practice in Nashville. He'd been instrumental in advancing phalloplasty surgery both on an aesthetic and micro-vascular level and came highly recommended for his skill, attitude, and bedside manner. The fact that he was also Greek scored big points with my mom. "Ooh, Shriny, I've got a good feeling about him," she said. "He's practically Armenian—it's meant to be!"

I was even more excited: Two weeks earlier I had zero options. Now I had an appointment with Dr. Michael Stephanides, a talented, experienced surgeon who was only one time zone away instead of three. And with Mom's immune system back to full capacity and her blood test results leukemia-free, she was able to fly with Dad and me to meet the man in person.

We were all in good spirits as we walked through the Nashville International Airport, taking in the country music paraphernalia and historic memorabilia decorating the walls. Then we got to baggage claim and discovered my suitcase was the only one that had arrived. To help keep my dad from losing it, I took care of filing the report with the lost baggage department and returned to my parents with two complimentary Dopp kits and the airline's promise that their missing luggage would be delivered to the hotel the next morning.

The unexpected delay had eaten up the time we would have had to check in and freshen up before my appointment, so we now needed to go straight to the doctor's office. This would have been fine had it not been for our next surprise: a stretch limo parked at the curb with our name on it.

"Jesus Christ," Dad huffed.

"Oh, Ed, lighten up," Mom shushed.

I gave the driver a smile and a wave and he came rushing over, eager to help take care of us. We were clearly not in Boston anymore.

"Is this all the luggage you have?" he asked, taking the handle of my suitcase, knowing full well three vacationing adults couldn't possibly get by on what fit inside. I nodded and after noting the sour look on my dad's face, he quickly changed gears.

"Now I know y'all ordered a sedan, but seeing there was three of you, we thought you'd be more comfortable in thisssssss," he said dramatically, adding a Vanna White arm flourish to emphasize the absurd length of the vehicle. Disappointed by our lackluster response, he quickly followed up with, "No extra charge." To make him feel better, Mom immediately began gushing over the extravagance of the limo as she climbed into the backseat. It worked. Soon he was smiling again.

Our lack of enthusiasm wasn't because we were ungrateful for the upgrade. It's just that we're not flashy people to begin with, so the last thing we wanted to do was pull into my doctor's office looking like rich assholes and, by extension, get charged out the wazoo for my surgery. Fortunately, the medical building had a rear entrance and we asked the driver to drop us there, only further disappointing him.

Walking into Orcutt Plastic Surgery Specialists felt more like walking onto the set of the TV series *Designing Women*. The waiting room was pure "Southern elegance" with its overstuffed upholstered furniture, chintz pillows, and accent tables in light washed wood and glass. But the warmth emanating from the room came largely from the nurses and staff. It may have been the Southern drawl, but everyone seemed so friendly. And when Dr. Stephanides came out to greet us and introduced himself simply as "Mike," I liked him immediately. It felt disrespectful to call him by his first name though, so I just started calling him "Doc."

If Doc's accent didn't betray his Greek heritage, his dark eyes and olive complexion were pretty good clues. He was around 5'10", fit from playing regular tennis, and despite his pepper-colored hair being flecked with quite a bit of salt, his flawless skin and mischievous grin made him seem ageless. His English was formal; he used very few contractions. He also spoke very quickly—when he got the chance. It was hard to get a word in with my mom going on about the similarities between Greek and Armenian food.

"Have you ever had paklava?" she asked him. "It's the Armenian version of baklava. We make it with cinnamon. I'll have to send you some, you'll looove it."

Doc escorted us down a corridor to his office, which, compared to the waiting room, looked oddly out of place: stark white walls, gray wall-to-wall carpeting, and a contemporary gray leather couch, behind which hung a painting of white stucco buildings overlooking the Mediterranean.

"That's Cyprus," he told us. "My homeland."

"And what, pray tell, is *that?*" I asked motioning toward the elephant in the room: a three-foot by five-foot painting of a naked woman with exceptionally large breasts lying on her side. It was on the floor propped up against the wall.

"Oh, a patient made that for me to thank me for doing her boob job. I don't know where to put it."

"How 'bout at home over your bed?" Dad suggested, laughing at his own joke.

Doc laughed too, and then we all spent the next ten minutes listening to Mom's unsolicited decorating advice. Finally Doc's nurse stuck her head inside the door to find out what all the laughter was about, which we took as a subtle cue to get down to business.

Unlike the other doctors I'd met with, Doc created a PowerPoint presentation to take us through the surgery. He began by speaking in general terms and then clicked to a slide that featured a grid like the one in the opening of the *Brady Bunch*. Only instead of Marcia, Greg, Peter, Jan, Bobby, Cindy, Mike, Carol, and Ann B. Davis as Alice, inside each square was a picture of a different penis. He asked us to determine which one was the fake—the one created by the procedure I was going to have. I could feel the tops of my ears turn red. Scrutinizing male genitalia with a parent on either side of you is awkward enough, let alone working with them as a team to pick the "imposter" out of a lineup.

And none of us guessed right. Turns out it was a trick question. They were all anatomical originals. The point was to illustrate there is no "right way" a penis should look. I understood where Doc was coming from, but I still pointed to the most stereotypical image on the screen and said, "I get it, but that's the one I want."

We spent another hour with Doc asking questions and discussing procedural details before nailing down a realistic timeframe for the first of what I learned would be six surgeries over two years. He asked me if I smoked, adding that if I did, I better quit because it inhibits the body's ability to heal.

"I don't smoke."

"Good. Smoking is the worst thing you can do to your body and I refuse to operate on anyone who smokes."

Again I assured him I was, in fact, a nonsmoker and that I couldn't stand even the smell of smoke. With that settled, I showed him my forearm. He echoed Dr. Laub's concerns about the hair growth but thought we could shoot for surgery in July—just three months away. Mom squeezed my leg. I was grinning uncontrollably but still trying not to get my hopes up; my Armo hair had screwed me plenty of times before. Doc said I should continue to do both electrolysis and laser on my arm and just laser on my groin.

Say *what* now?

"Ah . . . Dr. Laub didn't mention anything about needing to laser my *groin* . . ."

"Do you want a hairy penis?"

"No."

"Hairy balls?"

"No."

"Well then, you better get going on it."

"But I thought you just used skin from my abdomen and forearm?"

"Possibly the groin area too. I won't know until I see how your tissue responds. But we will definitely be using your labia for the balls."

I didn't know what was more horrifying: the thought of getting zapped with a laser "down there" or having a conversation about my labia in front of my parents. Doc assumed the former.

"Look, Chris, it is up to you. I am sensing you are a perfectionist and that you have a very specific idea of what you want aesthetically. I am just letting you know what you will have to go through to get it."

"Okay, gotcha."

I was relieved we were finally putting an end to this conversation.

"Besides," he added, "lots of guys have hairy balls."

Mom turned to me, "You don't want that. Get the laser."

Oh my god. Make it stop.

Dad mercifully changed the subject.

"So insurance doesn't cover this type of surgery at all?"

"No. Not usually. They consider it elective surgery—purely cosmetic and therefore unnecessary. But we lower our charges a bit and try to minimize your hospital stay to keep costs down—we have no control over what they charge. It's cheaper to stay at a four-star hotel. Many patients who come from out of town stay at the Hampton Suites or Extended Stay America so they can have a kitchen and not have to pay for room service. Where are you staying?"

"The Loews Vanderbilt Plaza," I mumbled, embarrassed.

"That's a nice hotel. And very close to here."

"Oh, good," Mom said. "We haven't been yet. We came straight from the airport."

"Ok, well, do you know where you're going?"

"We'll figure it out," Dad offered. "We don't want to take up any more of your time."

We all got up, exchanged pleasantries, and shook hands with Doc.

He escorted us back to the waiting area and told the receptionist he was going to walk us to our car and make sure we knew how to get to the hotel. The three of us froze. So much for our clean getaway.

"No, no, no, that's okay," Dad said. "Really, we're fine."

"I have to go see a patient at the hospital anyway. Come on, we'll go out the shortcut."

As we left the building, Mom promised to send Doc homemade paklava, while Dad and I prepared to be humiliated by the shiny black monstrosity now parked at the front entrance.

"Whoa, look at that thing. Someone famous must be here for a facelift," Doc joked.

"Nope, that would be us," I admitted as the driver ran around and opened the door, smiling. "They gave us a free upgrade. We're humiliated."

Doc laughed and, as we all climbed into the back of the limousine, asked the driver if he knew how to get to the Loews from here. The driver looked at him like he was high; you could see the hotel from the parking lot.

"Thanks, Doc. See you in July," I yelled out the tinted window. He waved and watched us slowly drive off. The conversation in the back of the limo went something like this:

Mom: I LOVE him, Shtiny!

Me: Me too.

Mom: He's like a long-lost cousin. I'll have to send him some paklava.

Dad: [Headshake combined with eye roll.]

Me: Did you like him, Dad?

Dad: Yes. Very much. He seems very competent and compassionate.

Mom: Did you see his hands? He has surgeon's hands—very delicate.

Me: And hairless. He barely had any hair on his arms either. Lucky bastard.

Mom: He didn't have one wrinkle on his face. Do you think
       he had work done?

Me and Dad (in unison): No.

Mom: How old do you think he is?

Me: I don't know . . . thirty-seven? Thirty-eight?

Dad: He's gotta be older than that. He has two kids.

Me: 40?

Mom: His wife is from Vermont, you know. We should bring
       her a Red Sox hat.

Things were looking up. We had a doctor we loved and a surgery date to shoot for. This was really going to happen! We celebrated by having drinks and listening to some live music at Tootsie's Orchid Lounge, a tourist staple in the honky-tonk section of downtown Nashville where Patsy Cline and Hank Williams Jr. once played. As I sat there sipping my Miller Lite, watching my dad watching my mom get hit on by a dancing, drunk man in his seventies, It struck me again how truly lucky I was.

And then I remembered about having to laser my groin.

••

"Oh, honey, I've seen it all."

That was Faye's response when I sheepishly told her about the additional area I'd need to have lasered.

"Don't be embarrassed. I've had gay guys come in all the time wanting their cock and balls done. I even did a guy's anus once."

Dear God.

While I waited for the numbing cream to take effect, Faye stepped out to assist Margaret with a treatment in the other room. She came back a half hour later singing a song by the Eagles and getting most of the lyrics wrong. I laughed and she suggested I not make fun of her singing when she was the one with the laser in her hand, then cackled to herself and started up the machine. I was lying on the bed with its back raised slightly. It was like lounging in a chaise by the pool. Only instead of being caressed by a relaxing summer breeze, I was being repeatedly electrocuted in the most sensitive of areas, each zap causing me to squeeze the armrests tighter and curse in ways I never knew possible. At one point, Margaret came running in to see what was going on and after getting an eyeful, promptly excused herself and closed the door behind her.

Faye kept asking if I wanted to stop and take a break but I instructed her, amid a flurry of f-bombs, to just get it over with. After roughly twelve agonizing minutes, it was. I had nearly torn off one of the armrests and was completely drenched in sweat. Faye asked if I wanted to wait a few minutes before doing my arm. *Shit. I'd forgotten all about that.* As I mentally prepared for round two of her torture session, I reminded myself that all this pain and suffering was going to pay off in the long run.

And it did. But due to unforeseen complications that my hairless urethra couldn't prevent, Doc's estimate of six surgeries over the course of two years was a bit off.

From 2002 to 2007, I had surgery twenty-two times.

If you break it down, that's roughly one procedure every three months. Some required multiple-night stays in the hospital and a few weeks' recovery in Nashville. Others I was able to knock out over a long weekend. Those "weekend wonders" were performed in Doc's office with me wide-awake, acting as his assistant. Once I was numb from the Novocain and the continual sight of my own blood, I had no problem handing him instruments, applying pressure with gauze, or holding my would-be shaft at a certain angle while he stitched, cut, or cauterized. These newfound medical skills were saving thousands of dollars in hospital bills.

In the end, my five-year quest for male genitalia would cost more than $100,000, not including travel. I was beyond fortunate my parents had the means to pay for my surgery. Lord knows I sure didn't. Nor do most people in my situation today. Again, this is why I'm one of only a small group of transgender men in this country who have chosen to "go all the way" when it comes to bottom surgery. As I've mentioned, the "deluxe model" doesn't come cheaply or easily. It's an expensive, painful, and time-consuming proposition with the potential for myriad complications and no guarantees when it comes to aesthetics or sensation. It's pretty freaking scary and oftentimes I felt like I was in what would have been Dante's tenth circle of hell. But I'd do it all over again if I had to. That feeling of finally being complete—of being who you really are—trumps *everything*.[5]

That said, many people who are transgender choose not to undergo surgery, even if they can afford it. There could be a number of reasons: pain, risk, fear, uncertain results, lack of support, or just being happy with their body the way it is and not feeling the need. Which brings me to an important point: You should *never* ask someone who is transgender if they have had or plan to have surgery. First, it's none of your business. Second, it's offensive because by asking that question you are implying that the person is not the gender they feel they are unless they alter their genitals. The fact is gender identity is not defined by what's inside your pants; it's defined by what's inside your brain. It's also something nobody questions or even thinks about unless it doesn't match the body they were born with. This is why people who are not transgender have so much trouble understanding what it's like to be in our shoes, and often why they are compelled to ask so many questions.

While many members of the transgender community consider the surgery topic off limits, I was very open about it. I didn't care if people knew I was having surgery. It was actually less stressful for me knowing I didn't have to hide it, especially at work. What was I going to do? Make up twenty-two different stories about why I would be out of the office for weeks at a time? It was a relief being able to be honest. I'd simply say, "I'm having surgery," and people would just say, "Ohhhhh," and kind of nod. When I'd come back from medical leave, everyone would ask me

---

5   Because gender dysphoria has recently been classified as a medical condition and not a mental disorder, more and more health insurance companies are providing coverage for gender reassignment procedures. (Some states, like Massachusetts, even mandate it.) Hopefully this will soon become accepted as standard medical protocol so that any transgender person who needs surgery can get it, regardless of financial ability.

how it went—more out of genuine concern than anything else—and wait for me to offer up whatever information I was willing to share.

Of course my close friends and family were privy to all the gory details—partly because I'm an over-sharer and partly because they were curious and wanted to know. I tried to explain the basic procedure in terms they'd understand, which was challenging because I was having difficulty understanding it myself. Doc took me through it at least three times, but I still couldn't process all the technical details—kind of like when I'm lost and someone is giving me directions that start to get complicated. I'll nod along, but if it takes more than three steps to get me back on track, I just stop listening.

So the simplest way I could describe the first stage of my phalloplasty surgery was that the doctor would use abdominal tissue and a skin graft from my hip to create a vertical tube resembling a suitcase handle. One end would be attached below the bellybutton and the other at the pubic bone. After three months I'd go back for the second stage of the procedure, in which the top part of the "handle" below the belly button would be detached so that it hung down, and voila! The shaft.

This sparked major discussion among my female friends who, upon finding out I'd have some control over the dimensions of my penis, felt compelled to weigh in. Aside from one assertion that "it's not the size of the wave but the motion of the ocean," most of the female input I received was that size did matter but length was not as important as girth.

"You definitely don't want the nickname 'needle dick,'" I was told.

"Go for the beer can!"

These comments led to an in-depth discussion with my doctor about penis size. I had read somewhere that the average penis was 3 to 3.5 inches long when flaccid and 5 to 5.5 inches when erect. Since my penis would remain the same length in both situations, I needed to take a one-size-fits-all approach. Doc said he would make the shaft six inches long to start and that he could make it up to two inches longer or shorter at a later stage. He said he couldn't make any promises on the girth as it would depend on my abdominal tissue and skin graft but assured me I would definitely not be called "needle dick." He added that most guys come in wanting huge penises and then end up coming back in to have them made smaller because it's too much to carry around all day—especially for patients who are vertically challenged (i.e., short) like me. Since my penis would be spending most of its time inside my pants, I was leaning more toward being average size than porn star size. Little did I know, Doc had other plans . . .

●●

Everything was dark. I could hear voices but couldn't make out words. The one with the Greek accent that was extremely chipper I knew belonged to my doctor. *That's right, I'm in the hospital.* I tried to open my eyes but again, the sandbags were back. *That must be the anesthesia kicking in.* Then I heard laughter and two voices I recognized as my parents.

"What's so funny?" I mumbled, straining to open my eyes.

"Heeeey, Chris. You're awake," Doc said cheerfully.

"Hi, Shtinc," I heard Mom say and then felt a light kiss on my forehead.

"Are they taking me in now?" I asked, catching a blurry glimpse of the three of them standing over me like Mount Rushmore before my eyes drooped closed again.

"You're all done," Dad said warmly. I felt his hand pat my leg.

"You were in there six hours," Mom added.

"I gave you eight inches!" Doc announced.

I recall muttering something about not needing a kickstand, which got everyone laughing, and then felt a draft below my waist from what I presumed were blankets being lifted off of me.

"Jesus Christ!" I heard my dad say. "That thing is bigger than mine!"

●●

By day three I was finally getting some quality sleep. The reason? I was no longer forced to wear auto-inflating support hose that tightened around my legs like a blood pressure cuff every twenty minutes. Even better, I had moved out of the hospital and into the Loews Vanderbilt Hotel. The general manager gave us a special medical discount rate on a two-bedroom suite because we were going to be there for a few weeks and would be spending a lot of money on room service. The upscale accommodations my parents sprang for definitely helped ease the pain, but nothing helped my convalescence more than having my mom there to take care of me. For the first few days, I could barely sit up or get out of bed on my own. She made sure I was taking all the right meds at the right times, changing my dressings, and monitoring the fluid level in my drain tubes. She filled in concerned family members, friends, and coworkers on how I was doing when I couldn't, and played cards and watched movies with me all day despite the way I smelled. She even walked the eight blocks to Arby's in the July Nashville heat to answer my craving for a junior roast beef. I don't know what I would've done without her. It was a long two weeks for both of us. We were starving for other human interaction. Fortunately, I had a doctor who made house calls.

"Most of my patients stay at the Extended Stay America for fifty-two dollars a night," Doc said, eyeballing the dining room table positioned directly under the vaulted windows.

"They're giving us a discounted medical rate," I offered, embarrassed. After the prior incident with the limo, something told me he wasn't too surprised by our digs. What surprised us, however, were Doc's daily visits. I figured Mom would be shuttling me back and forth to his clinic. But instead, he'd phone in "between boob jobs" or "on the way to a facelift" to see how I was doing and let me know when he would be by to make sure everything was healing okay. Every day he'd show up to check on me, usually in his scrubs or tennis gear and always chewing gum. (What was that about?) Sometimes he'd stay for a snack or a drink. I got the feeling he enjoyed the visits as much as I did. He gave me his cell number and told me to call it anytime. I gave him a key to my room and joked that things were moving too fast.

But on day seven, when he finally told me I could shower, it was I who couldn't move fast enough. Washing off a week's worth of stank was the turning point in my recovery. I was a new person. I just had to get used to the sight of the eight-inch flesh handle protruding from my abdomen.

Sadly, I barely got the chance.

SO MUCH FOR THOSE EIGHT INCHES

October 15, 2002

There's nothing worse than the smell of burning flesh. Especially when it's your own. In this case, the singeing was not an accident: The abdominal scarring from my hysterectomy had blocked adequate blood supply to my would-be penis. As a result, the tissue became necrotic, and two months post-surgery I found myself in Doc's office watching him cut and cauterize away a good six inches of the precious eight he'd created. I don't know which of us was more upset.

"I can feel that!" I shouted at one point, causing him to stop and inject me with more Novocain. While I was relieved to avoid the routine and expense of another hospital admission, undergoing this two-and-a-half-hour procedure while totally conscious had its own drawbacks. Lying there covered in bloody paper sheets I looked like the victim of a horrible murder—only I was still alive and assisting in my own mutilation.

"Hold this gauze here," Doc said. "I'm going to stitch up this nub . . . I think I can save the tissue."

I tried not to look while he quickly and masterfully glided the navy blue sutures in and out, and when he tied the final knot I looked down at my new miniature "Frankendick." I wanted to cry.

"Don't worry, when you come back next month I'll take care of it. You still have enough tissue for me to rebuild it—it was too big anyway."

That last part, while probably true, didn't make me feel any better. As if things couldn't get any worse, once I washed myself clean and slipped my boxers back on, I noticed the shadow of my silhouette on the wall.

"Ah, what am I supposed to do about this?"

Doc turned to face me. "About what?"

"THIS."

I turned to the side, to better accentuate my profile.

"What?"

"What do you mean *what*? This two-inch hard-on you've left me with for the next four weeks!"

We were both laughing now.

"Put your pants back on—no one will be able to tell." I put my loose-fit Levi's back on and turned to the side again.

"It's still there!"

Doc was doubled over laughing, still trying to talk me out of the fact that I had a permanent mini-erection. "Come on, we'll ask one of the girls."

We left the examining room and went down the hall, where one of the nurses was filing paperwork.

"Do you notice anything funny about Chris?" Doc asked her.

She looked at me from top to bottom, her eyes widening when they reached my crotch.

"Ah, yeah. That he has a hard-on. Are you sending him off to catch his plane like that?"

"He's sending me off for a month like this!"

"Now don't get excited," Doc joked.

"Thanks to you, I can't help it."

"Untuck your shirt," the receptionist chimed in. "That's what all the boys in high school used to do."

"Yes, yes. That will work," Doc confirmed, as though speaking from experience.

So that's what I did and would continue to do for the next four weeks.

Despite all the joking, I was devastated. And Doc knew it. When I called to let him know I got through airport security without a male assist, he reassured me with confidence that this was just a setback and everything would be fine.

Famous last words.

••

The main thing I remember about my "rebuilding" surgery was waking up in recovery and puking my brains out—much to the shock and dismay of my sister Wendy, who had come to Nashville to take care of me in place of my mom.

Normally one spends maybe thirty to forty-five minutes in recovery. My nausea was so extreme, I was in there for three hours. And every time I lurched forward to hurl into that pink basin, I had major pain in my abdomen from the surgery. Just before 5:00 p.m., Doc came in to warn me that the recovery room would be closing and if I wasn't well enough to leave, the nurses were going to make me spend the night in the hospital. I looked at him and Wendy and said, "Get me out of here."

It was like a scene from *Weekend at Bernie's*: one of them pulling up my hospital pants, the other slipping my arms through the sleeves of my button-down shirt . . . me slumped over them like I was dead, head lolling to the side. Occasionally I barfed into a plastic bag, my only sign of life. When I was finally dressed, Wendy held me up while Doc filled out the discharge papers and announced to the two suspect nurses how much better I felt and that I was ready to go. They gave him the hairy eyeball as he quickly wheeled me out of recovery, down a long maze of corridors, and straight out the exit, Wendy jogging behind. When we got outside the hospital doors, Doc hit the brake on the wheelchair and told us to wait while he pulled his car around. He had volunteered to drive us back to the hotel so we wouldn't have to rent a car or get a cab. His black Saab convertible came to a screeching halt right by the curb in front of us.

"I put the top down so you would have some fresh air. Please don't throw up in my car. I can't stand the sight or smell. It makes me sick."

"You're a surgeon," I said, struggling to get out of the wheelchair.

"I know. Blood I can take."

Wendy helped me to the car door, while Doc pushed the passenger seat forward so she could squeeze into the back. He saw the surprised looks on both our faces then immediately apologized for the mess, shoving aside empty Pepsi cans, dirty tennis clothes, and remnants of whatever snacks his four-year-old daughter had been eating back there. When he flipped the seat back for me, I saw the situation up front was no better.

"Am I gonna need a tetanus shot after this ride?"

"What? Is it that bad?" he asked genuinely while helping me slide in without bending at my waist too much.

"Oh, no," I replied, kicking aside the trash around my feet. As he closed my door and went around to the driver's side, I noticed two fresh foil packs of gum jammed into one of the cup holders and in the other, a half-empty pack of cigarettes. *Aha! That's why he's always chewing gum . . . to mask his hypocritical smoker's breath.* I got a whiff of the dirty ashtray and threw up a little in my mouth.

Doc pulled up in front of the two large lion statues that guarded the main entrance of the Loews Vanderbilt and waved off the valet who wasn't quite sure what to make of me. He and the guests inside the hotel lobby were treated to a showing of *Weekend at Bernie's II* as Wendy and Doc once again propped me up on either side and walked me to the elevator bank where, ironically, there was an old-time movie theater popcorn machine popping away. I was still nauseated and couldn't stand up or think straight but damn, that popcorn smelled good.

When I woke up the next morning in the comfort of my king-size bed, the nausea was finally gone. It was then that I took stock of my body and what shape I'd been left in. I recognized the familiar feeling of a binder, only this time it wasn't around my chest but around my abdomen. There were two drains pinned to it, one on each side of my waist, and even though my groin area was covered in dressings I could tell "stubby" wasn't much bigger than he was before surgery, which led me to believe things did not go according to plan. When Doc came by a few hours later, he re-explained what happened during the four-hour procedure. Apparently I didn't retain the information the first time around because I was too busy puking.

"Do you want the good news or the bad news first?" he asked.

"Ah, I'll take the bad news."

"I couldn't save the tissue. But I dropped the base of your penis and gained some tissue there. And I still think you have enough tissue in your abdominal and groin areas for me to build a decent-size shaft when you come back in January."

"Is that the good news?"

"No. The good news is I gave you a tummy tuck."

"You what?"

"That's the bonus of having a phalloplasty. I do that for all my patients to minimize the scarring from the first procedure. That's why you have those drains. They'll come out in five days and you'll need to wear that binder for four weeks, but after that you'll have a nice flat stomach."

"And no scars?"

"You'll have one thin horizontal scar below your waistline. But that's a lot better than what you had before."

"I'll say."

"Any other questions before I go?"

"Yeah. What's with the cigarettes in the car, Mister 'Smoking-is-the-worst-thing-you-can-do-to-your-body-and-I-refuse-to-operate-on-anyone-who-smokes'?"

He stared back at me with a guilty grin. "I plan to quit."

CATHY & JARED

January 2003

As prepared as I was with questions prior to surgery, there was always something I either forgot to ask or didn't know enough to ask. This meant varying degrees of unwelcome surprises (with the exception of a tummy tuck) on my road to recovery.

Such was the case with Cathy and Surgery #4.

While I knew Cathy would be with me during my time in Nashville, I was not expecting her to accompany me on the plane back to Boston. Nor did I anticipate she'd be staying with me for three more weeks. Yet there she was, 24/7. I couldn't shake her. Everywhere I went, she went. Home, work, bars, restaurants. She really cramped my style. I knew she was there to help me, but "Cathy the Catheter" was getting on my nerves.

Surgery #4 consisted of a vaginectomy (yes, it was as horrible as it sounds) and the creation of a urethral extension, which would eventually allow me to pee standing up. While I was told I'd need a catheter "post-surgery," I assumed that meant the days I'd be in the hospital. (Note to self: Always ask for specifics.)

After three days I was released from the hospital but not from Cathy. She was converted to a portable bag attached to my left thigh via an elastic band that was constantly pinching my leg hair. I likened the quick random bursts of pain to stepping on a Lego barefoot. When Cathy was empty, you couldn't really tell she was there, hiding under my baggy pants. But when she was full, it looked like I had a kilo of coke strapped to my thigh.

When I got to the hotel, Jill was waiting for me. I introduced her to Cathy and the three of us spent the next seven days ordering room service and watching pay-per-view movies and *Golden Girls* reruns. On day eight, I packed my suitcase and waited for Doc to swing by for my final checkup. He showed up with a box of medical supplies he'd swiped from the hospital and a bunch of instructions on what to do with them. I was following along fine until he got to the spare catheter bag.

"Ha. Ha," I said sarcastically.

He smiled, then looked at me, confused. "What?"

"You're serious?"

"What do you mean?"

"You're not taking this thing *out* before I go??"

"No, you can take it out yourself in four weeks—maybe three."

"WHAT?"

"It's no big deal. You just pull it out. I'll talk you through it over the phone."

"I have to go to work like this?"

"Wear your baggy jeans; no one will be able to tell."

I sat there shaking my head, right hand stretched across my furrowed brow. Doc broke the silence. "At least I'm not sending you on the plane with a hard-on."

While I made it through security without a pat down, I didn't make it through the three-hour flight without having to empty Cathy. Twice. This did not bode well for going stealth at the office. I started doing the math in my head. Average workday? Ten hours. That meant I'd have to conceal a pant leg full of urine at least six times a day.

The first few days I sat closest to the door at every meeting so when I stood up to leave I wouldn't have to walk past a conference room full of people with a giant bulge on my thigh. But as the days went on I cared less and less. I began openly referring to Cathy in the office and talking about how much I hated her. Soon it was a running joke among friends and coworkers.

"How's Cathy?" they'd ask.

"Ugh," I'd groan. "I'm so sick of that bitch."

When making plans, friends would ask if Cathy could come or just tell me to bring her along. One out of every four times I'd answer my phone, the voice on the other end would open with, "Is Cathy there?"

"No," I'd say. "Her phone privileges are revoked for repeatedly pinching my leg hair."

After eighteen days Cathy and I finally had it out. We were at my parents' house for Sunday dinner, and while standing at the sink rinsing my plate, I felt something warm running down my leg *inside* my pants. I looked down to find I was standing in the middle of an expanding yellow puddle.

Fucking Cathy!

I pulled my pants down; she had sprung a leak! I didn't know what to do. I yelled for my mom who stopped short when she saw me.

"What are you doing?"

"My catheter's leaking. What should I do?"

"Don't you have a spare bag?"

"Not on me!"

At this point Jill came in with more dishes from the table. She took one look at me with my pants around my ankles standing in a pool of urine and burst out laughing. Mom ordered her to get a Ziploc bag out of the drawer while I apologized profusely.

"You couldn't have done this in your own kitchen?" Mom griped, mopping up my pee.

"Sorry, Mom. I couldn't help it. At least you have a tile floor."

Jill handed her a sandwich bag. Mom looked at it, annoyed. "What am I supposed to do with this?"

"Oh, right," Jill cackled, exchanging it for the one-gallon size.

Now we were all laughing.

"What's going on in there?" Dad shouted from the dining room.

"Cathy's a whore!" Mom shouted back.

●●

While Cathy and I split up after just under a month, my relationship with Jared lasted much longer.

I'd finally had surgery to insert the tissue expander, or balloon, into my nearly hairless forearm. Over the course of four months I was to inject it with enough saline to fill a twenty-ounce Coke bottle. (I'll let you sit with that for a second.) The idea, as Dr. Laub had explained four years earlier, was that as the balloon gets bigger, the skin stretches to cover the increased surface area of the arm—kind of like what happens to a woman's belly during pregnancy. This "extra skin" was what would be used to make my urethral extension.

The needles I had to use to inject the saline were much larger and way more intimidating than the ones I used to inject myself with testosterone, and the process was a lot more challenging to pull off one-handed. To locate the injection site I had to feel for the metal port under my skin. I'd then draw a circle around it in pen, close my eyes, and hope for the best. The first time, I had Doc on speakerphone talking me through it. The rest of the times I had Jill or Straubs do it.

I'd scheduled this part of the surgery during the coldest months so I could hide what was going on under layers of winter clothing. But as it turned out, even my bulkiest sweater was no match for my inflatable forearm. When I noticed coworkers staring at the bulge in my sleeve, I told them it was a sub sandwich I was saving for later. So naturally, I named my arm "Jared" after the Subway spokesperson.

Unlike Subway Jared who recently had a major fall from grace, my Jared was extremely popular—way more popular than Cathy. He had a much better personality. He was always waving to people and everyone was always happy to see him. I responded to invitations with Jared as my "Plus 1." And my friends would always set an extra place for him at the dinner table. We became close over those four months, but our parting was inevitable. The time had come for him to serve a higher purpose.

THE BIG ONE

June 10, 2003

Ten and a half hours. That's how long it took Doc and his partner to build me a penis with outdoor plumbing and eventual sensation—the latter of which involved transplanting an artery, vein, and nerve from my forearm to my groin. I woke up in the ICU a bit lonely without Jared but comforted by the sight of what looked to be a giant "thumbs-up" wrapped in gauze between my legs. Then I vomited all over myself.

Enter Bonnie, the ICU nurse assigned to take care of me for the next twenty-four hours. "Ugh, now look what you've done," she barked, stripping off my puke-covered blanket. "If you have to throw up, use this." She held up the familiar pink basin, then set it on the bedside cart completely out of my reach.

At this point my dad tentatively walked in. Judging by the expression on his face, I didn't look so good. He came over and stood by my bed, wedging himself between my IV stand and the unreachable cart.

"They told me you were awake," he said, holding my hand.

"Can you grab me that basin?" Time for round two.

While I hurled, he glanced around nervously and then managed to get Nurse Bonnie's attention.

"Do you have anything bigger he can use . . . a bucket maybe?"

"No," she snapped. "That's what we use."

Dad narrowed his eyes at her, then looked back at me. "What's her problem?"

"I don't know."

"You were in there for over ten hours."

"That's probably why I'm so sick. The longer you're under anesthesia, the worse it is."

"Doc said he'd be by soon and told me I could sit with you for a bit." Dad looked around the tiny room. No guest chairs. Just my bed and a bunch of monitors, one of which was connected directly to my penis.

That was the real reason I was in ICU. My penis was on suicide watch. It needed continuous blood circulation for twenty-four hours after surgery for the tissue to survive, so it was hooked up to a Doppler machine that had to be checked every hour for a regular pulse. I looked through the glass partition at Bonnie, who was now chitchatting with a coworker.

At least the machine was doing its job.

Dad opened the glass door and politely asked Bonnie if there was a chair she could bring in so he could sit with me. She told him he wasn't allowed and that he'd already stayed too long and needed to leave. I thought Dad was going to explode but he calmly informed her that my doctor had given him permission. She told him doctors don't have that authority and that he had to leave. That did it.

"I'm going to sit with my son!" he shouted.

"Heeey, what's going on in here?" Doc had arrived right on cue.

Bonnie jumped in. "He asked for a chair and I was just telling him that no one is allowed to sit with a patient in ICU."

"I think you know that this patient is a special case," Doc said. "He's not at risk of dying, his penis is. I told his father he could sit with him."

She continued arguing with Doc until he finally just left the room. Seconds later he came back carrying a small plastic chair and plunked it next to my bed. Bonnie glared at him and stomped back behind the glass. Doc smiled at us.

"I have two other patients to check on. I'll be back in an hour. Try not to kill her."

When he returned I was mid-puke. He turned his back until I was done. "I can't stand the sight of throw up," he explained to Dad.

"You're a *doctor*," Dad said, laughing.

"I know, I know."

As Doc began giving Bonnie instructions for my care, Dad said his goodbyes and promised to be back in the morning. After he left, I tuned into the conversation going on at the foot of my bed. Bonnie was arguing with Doc, refusing to follow his instructions. He raised his voice, which I'd never heard him do, and she stomped back behind the partition. I looked at him fearfully.

"Don't worry. She'll do what I told her. You'll be fine. I'll come back after my first surgery in the morning."

"Okay. But before you go can you leave a basin on my bed in case I have to throw up again? I keep asking her and she won't bring me one."

He opened the glass door. "Bonnie, we need a puke basin in here." He then came back over to my bedside. "If you need her during the night, just press the call button."

"What call button?"

Just then Bonnie appeared wearing her familiar scowl.

"You didn't show him the call button?" Doc said in disbelief.

"Yes, I did. He was probably out of it and just doesn't remember."

I glared at her.

"It's right behind your head," she said and finally handed me the basin. I fell asleep clutching it. But when I woke up at 3:00 a.m. with another wave of nausea, it was gone. I raised my head and shoulders as much as I could and scanned the bedside cart. It wasn't there. I peered through the glass partition. Bonnie's back was to me. Again she was chatting with two other nurses at the desk. I felt the bile rising and knew it was only a matter of seconds. I reached for the call button and pushed it. No reaction. I pushed it again and again. Still nothing.

I threw up all over myself.

I lay there in my own vomit, screaming for help, but to no avail. I tried adding arm-waving to my attention-getting repertoire, hoping one of the other nurses might notice me, but my left arm was largely immobile due to the Jared-ectomy, and the range of motion in my right arm was limited by my hand's attachment to the IV. In a last-ditch effort, I was able to reach the plastic cup by my bed and throw it at the partition. It didn't get close. I gave up and after a few minutes eventually drifted back to sleep.

••

"Christopher, wake up."

There was a split second when I forgot where I was. Then I opened my eyes and saw my nemesis. "You threw up all over yourself again."

"You took away my basin," I said icily.

"I didn't think you still needed it. You should've pressed the call button."

"I did. It doesn't work."

"What are you talking about?" She reached over and pushed the button a few times. "Huh, you're right. It's not plugged in."

"I was yelling 'help' at the top of my lungs and trying to get your attention. You left me lying here in my own puke for"—I looked up at the clock on the wall—"forty-five minutes."

"Well, you're fine now," she said apathetically and left the room with my stained linens under her arm. She returned with fresh bedding, a clean jonnie, and, to my relief, a puke basin. There was not one ounce of tenderness in her actions as she changed me and while I didn't want to believe it, I wondered if she was treating me differently because I was transgender. There's no way a nurse with such a callous and demeaning bedside manner would be allowed to care for ICU patients, right? I mean, she couldn't possibly treat everybody like this. I fell asleep seething.

I was moved out of the ICU late in the afternoon and was relieved to find the nurses on the sixth floor to be the complete opposite of Bonnie. They took outstanding care of me over the next six days, checking my penis's pulse every two to three hours and constantly making sure I was comfortable and had everything I needed. Doc also came by regularly with DVDs and Dairy Queen.

Devouring my DQ combo meal, I reminded myself that Bonnie was an outlier. Everyone from Doc and all the other nurses to the entire staff at the Loews Vanderbilt Hotel had treated me with nothing but sensitivity and kindness, often going above and beyond to make my medical stays as painless as possible. How many doctors do you know who chauffeur their patients around, let alone take them out to dinner? When was the last time a hotel manager offered to pick up groceries for you, or room service added a special dessert to your tray because they thought you could use some cheering up? I vowed not to let Bonnie's appalling behavior overshadow that of all the amazing people I'd come to know over the last few years. When it came to my Nashville family, she was the redheaded stepchild.

That said, I didn't want any other patient to be treated the way Bonnie treated me. So while recovering at the hotel, I crafted a detailed letter to the head of ICU. Apparently, there must have been other complaints filed against her, because shortly after I got home to Boston, Doc called to tell me that Bonnie had been suspended. Rumor had it she was last seen carrying out her belongings in a pink kidney-shaped puke basin.

Sweet justice: another reason to get my drink on.

•

The "big" surgery was over and done with and I was headed to Meek's house with a bottle of Grey Goose to celebrate with my crew. As usual, the girls drank their wine upstairs and the guys brought their drinks down to "Lou's basement," Meek's husband's domain. It was cold and damp and had a sump pump jutting up from the middle of the concrete floor, but it also had a dartboard and refrigerator filled with Coors Light. I can't remember how the topic came up—nor could anyone else (we'd been boozing it up pretty good)—but from what I can recall, one of the guys asked me how the surgery went, and from there the group wanted to know if I thought "it" looked real. I said something like, "You guys would know better than I would. Wanna see it?" They were all like *yeah yeah, let's see it,* so I whipped it out—something I never thought I'd do no matter how much vodka I'd consumed.

I only had it out for a few seconds and in that time I remember wide eyes, a few gasps, and maybe a "holy shit!" or two, all of which I took to be a good sign. They agreed Doc had done a great job—it looked incredibly real. I didn't get that they also thought it was big until Straubs' husband thanked me for making him feel inadequate and Meek's brother-in-law shouted, "Damn my Irish DNA!"

I won't lie: It felt good to know my buddies were envious of the size of my penis. The fact that it was still swollen from surgery? Yeah, I kept that to myself.

A PAIN IN THE BALLS

November 2003

One thing everybody knows about Straubs' husband, Lars, is that he's proud of his Scandinavian roots; the clogs are a dead giveaway. But what only a select few know is that one week a year he has access to a villa on St. Barts. This year, he and Straubs invited a group of us to join them during "their week" in November. We all jumped on it, as we'd heard about their previous trips and seen photos of pool parties, tropical drinks, and sunsets on the beach. When the time came, however, I was more stressed than excited.

Six months earlier my job situation had changed drastically. The anti-tobacco industry account I'd been working on cut their budget in half and my other main account, Monster.com, had been bought by a holding company that left Arnold for an agency on Madison Avenue. A few days later, I got a call from Alan, one of my favorite group creative directors, asking me to come see him in his office. *Dead man walking*, I thought as I headed down the hall to his corner of the floor. He was wearing khaki shorts and an old Boy Scout uniform shirt boasting a wide array of merit badges, pretty much the norm for him. I'd worked in Alan's group for three years and loved his quirky personality, genuineness, and sensitivity. He cared about every person on his team and their careers. So when I saw his pained smile, I braced myself for bad news.

I nervously eyeballed his Shriner's Club vintage fez collection while he closed his office door—something he rarely did. Before he could say anything I asked him if I was getting canned. He said no, but that finance was all over the creative department like "yaks in heat" and that there were going to be layoffs and then a reorg. They had two roles in mind for me, both in his group, and I could take my pick.

Option 1: Retain my title as Associate Creative Director and work on Citizens Bank.

Option 2: Get promoted to Creative Director and co-run the McDonald's account.

While I was relieved to still have a job, I wasn't excited for either option. First, I'd no longer be with my partner, Mike, with whom I had great creative chemistry and an even better friendship. Second, both accounts offered less of a creative opportunity than what I'd been previously working on. The bank was an up-and-comer, but it was still a bank. How far was I really going be able to move the needle creatively? McDonald's was a great national brand with an amazing creative track record, but the work Arnold did was regional, retail, and low budget. It was the second largest account at the agency and hadn't won a creative award in years. I asked Alan if I could have the weekend to think about it.

Of course I took the promotion and went with McDonald's. I'm not an idiot. I just needed time for the shock to wear off. A promotion meant a raise, and also that I'd have control over the work. Plus, I loved their fries.

In keeping with my Type A+ personality, I outlined a five-year plan for myself, during which I would complete the following steps: elevate the level of creativity; get spots featured on the agency reel; make it a fun account that creatives wanted to work on; and win awards. A tall order but I knew I could do it. That summer the national "I'm lovin' it" campaign was introduced, and I was responsible for Arnold's first national McDonald's assignment: to develop a library of promotional TV spots in the new campaign direction for agencies throughout the country to use with their own local retail messaging.

No pressure.

In the middle of all this, I'd undergone another surgery: Balls—
Stage 1. Tissue expanders (smaller versions of the one in my arm) had
been inserted you know where, and filled with twenty ccs on each side.
I was walking like I'd just come back from a three-day trail ride, and
instead of subsiding, the pain was getting worse. Soon the expander
in my right "ball" eroded through the skin, necessitating another trip
to Nashville to have it removed. Now, with just two days to go before
my flight to St. Barts, I sat in the middle of a never-ending production
meeting with my left "ball" killing me. I shifted in my seat and felt a
strange wet sensation between my legs.

This can't be good.

I gave the producer the "wrap it up" signal and she cut off the
director's long-winded speech recapping his vision for our spots that
he'd obviously come up with five minutes before the call. I bolted for
the men's room. Once safely inside a stall, I unzipped and gasped. It
looked like the Wonder Bread factory had blown up in my pants. After
using a whole roll of toilet paper to mop myself up, I snuck back to my
office, grabbed my stuff, and ran for the elevator. As soon as I got home
I called Doc and described what I saw. He told me it sounded like I had
a major yeast infection from the remaining tissue expander and that it
would need to be removed as well.

"Can I still go to St. Barts?"

"Yes, I'll prescribe you some antibiotics, but you know what that
means."

"What?"

"No drinking for a week."

"But I'm on vaca—"

"Okay, limit yourself to two drinks a day. No more than that."

"You're such a pushover. Can I go swimming?"

"Yes. Not in a pool though. Only the beach. The salt water will help
you heal, so feel free to go skinny dipping."

"Not gonna happen, but thanks for the tip."

"Have a good vacation, hee hee."

Years later Doc would *hee hee* me again during another balls-related off-hours emergency call. I was going to Baltimore for the Preakness, and the night before my flight I'd developed an infection that was accompanied by a raging case of jock itch—my first. Doc again prescribed antibiotics and a two-drink maximum and suggested I pick up a can of Lotrimin anti-fungal spray to combat the itch. Of course there was only one size available at the twenty-four-hour CVS and it definitely did not meet the TSA's carry-on requirements. I was on a tight schedule and didn't want to check my bag, so I took a chance. Sure enough, it was pulled for a search. The young TSA agent with extra-long acrylic fingernails held up my duffle and asked for its owner. I raised my hand.

"Do you have something liquid in here?

"No . . . "

She unzipped my bag and pulled out the value-size can of Lotrimin AF.

"You can't take this on board," she reprimanded.

"But I *need* it," I begged.

It was then that she actually read the can, which was emblazoned with the words *SUPER SIZE* and *CURES MOST JOCK ITCH* in neon yellow. Trying to stifle her laughter, she took pity on me. "Okay . . . well, we'll have to ask him. He's my supervisor." She pointed to an extremely large dude sitting at the wanding station, eyelids at half-mast. Judging from his thunder thighs, I was guessing he was no stranger to jock itch and might be inclined to help me out.

"Can he take this through?" she asked.

Moving only his eyes, Thunder looked at the can, then at me with an expression that said *I feel for you, man* and gave the nod. But before I could do my victory dance I was told I had to wait for the can to be dusted for explosive residue. My anti-fungal spray was displayed and scrutinized by three different members of security before it was deemed safe to carry aboard. Humiliating, yes. But in the scheme of things, a small price to pay for guydom.

MY DOCTOR THE MATCHMAKER

Martin Luther King Day, 2005

From: Chris Edwards <cedwards@arn.com>
To: Sean Vernaglia <svernaglia@arn.com>
Date: January 18th, 2005 2:40 PM EDT
Re: OOO: AUTOMATED REPLY

Thanks for your email. I will be out of the office Jan 17th–31st.
For all things McDonald's, please contact Bob Pye.
He'll be hiding under his desk.

While my co-creative director was dreading it, I was looking forward to my "Martin Luther King Day surgery" for a few reasons:

1. I was finally getting my balls.
2. This was going to be my twelfth and final procedure.
3. It would allow me some much-needed time off. (You know it's bad when you'd take surgery over work.)

The operation lasted roughly three hours. The tissue expanders were removed and a silicone testicular implant was inserted along with a pump that would enable the penile implant to become erect. I was back at the hotel for a week of recuperation—this time by myself. Doc had told me the recovery would be relatively easy—just limited movement for the first few days—so I decided to go solo. I needed to decompress anyway. Doc felt bad that I didn't have anyone to keep me company, especially since this was a crazy busy time for him and he couldn't hang out with me as much as usual. I assured him I would be fine by myself, that it was not his job to entertain me, and that I planned to enjoy my time relaxing with my two friends: On-Demand and Room Service. Later that evening he called to check on me and out of nowhere . . .

"Soooo, Chris, do you remember Karen Marie from my office? You met her two times ago. She's the aesthetician I had test out our new laser on your birth mark?"

"The hot one with long dark hair? Ah, yeah. I remember her."

"I gave her your cell number."

"WHAT?"

"She's going to call you."

"Are you insane?" This girl was completely out of my league, and I was in no condition to go out on a date with anyone—let alone her.

"She thought you were cute and asked my nurse what you were seeing me for. When she found out you were one of my gender patients, she couldn't believe it. She asked me how long you were in town. I told her you were here by yourself for a few more days and suggested she call you and take you out one night."

"Doc!"

"What? It doesn't have to be romantic. It'll be nice to have a friend in Nashville when you come back next time."

"This is my last surgery."

"No, I couldn't do a few things, so you have to come back. I'll tell you about it tomorrow."

"I'm going to kill you."

"Okay, bye, hee hee."

Two nights later, I waited nervously in the hotel lobby, peering out the glass doors, occasionally setting off the sensor and making them slide open. Judging from the sudden bursts of cold air, I'd guessed it was somewhere between forty and forty-five degrees outside. Downright balmy for a New Englander like myself.

I didn't really know what I was looking for. I had no idea what kind of car she'd be driving. I wasn't even sure I'd recognize her. I mean, it'd been six months since she zapped my cheek with the laser. I did remember her having beautiful brown, almond-shaped eyes and long dark hair. She was probably my height, but she'd been wearing high heels—the kind with the strap that went around the ankle. I remember thinking they were a bit racy for the office and the white lab coat that covered up whatever else she had on. I wondered what she'd be wearing tonight and what she'd think of my outfit: the same roomy Levi's and charcoal gray zip front sweatshirt I'd packed for every surgery. I didn't bring any nice clothes, as I wasn't expecting to leave the hotel, never mind go on any dates while I was here. And was this even a date? Or just a pity party arranged by Doc?

I saw someone I suspected might be her get out of a Jeep Grand Cherokee and head toward the entrance. I took a step forward to get a better look and again accidentally activated the automatic doors. They slid open and she smiled.

"Chris?"

"Karen Marie," I said, smiling back. She was shorter than me without her heels on and she looked even tinier under her puffy winter coat, hat, and scarf.

"I wasn't sure if you'd remember me," she said.

"How could I forget?" I said back. "You lasered my face."

She laughed.

She opened the passenger door for me, stood patiently while I gingerly negotiated my way into the front seat, then closed the door behind me. This gender-role reversal made me feel completely emasculated, but it didn't seem to faze her. She started up the engine and turned right onto West End Avenue. We were going to see the movie *Sideways*, which had gotten great reviews. Normally I had no trouble striking up conversation; I could talk to a brick wall. But I was nervous and in no mood to go out with somebody new. I struggled for an opener.

"I Fandangoed," I said.

"You what?"

"Fandangoed—you know, ordered the tickets in advance online?"

"Oh, I've never done that."

"Me neither. I guess we'll see if it works."

That pretty much summed up my clever banter from the evening. I was relieved when the movie finally started so I wouldn't have to stress over making more small talk. We just weren't clicking. I'd make a joke, and she wouldn't get it. She'd say something, and I'd misunderstand what she meant. It was nice to be out for a few hours and I thought she was very sweet, but I was happy to get back to my hotel room.

The next afternoon I got a call from Doc.

"What is your favorite food?" he asked quickly.

"Who is this?" I joked.

"I'm here with Karen Marie. She's going to take you out for dinner tonight. She was thinking sushi, but I told her you only eat burgers and pizza."

"Well, I like burgers and pizza but I also eat other things."

"Sushi?"

"No, not sushi."

"He says pizza!" Doc yelled over his shoulder.

"I didn't say that. Can you please not—"

"I'll put her on."

"What? No, don't—"

"Hi, Chris. I hear you're tired of hotel food. I'll take you out for pizza tonight. I know a good place."

"Okay. You really don't have to."

"No, I want to. Is seven okay?"

"Let me check my schedule. Yup."

"Ha, okay, I'll pick you up out front."

••

The pizza place, appropriately named Christopher's (I bought a t-shirt), was right up my alley: a local dive that served up old-school pies and great music. It reminded me of one of my favorite pizza joints back home. We sat down across from each other in an uncomfortable wooden booth and Karen Marie immediately began removing her hat, scarf, and puffy coat. I noticed this time she was also wearing gloves. I asked her if she was wearing long underwear too.

"Nooooo," she said making a face at me. She was starting to get my sense of humor. She eyeballed me, accessory-less in my unzipped fall jacket. "Aren't you cold?"

"Have you ever been to New England in January?"

She told me she'd never been to New England but that she'd be going to New York for a conference in the spring. Then asked how far away it was from Boston.

Hmmm . . . interesting.

When the waiter came to take our order, Karen Marie informed me that Doc said I was allowed only one beer because I was on antibiotics. To make the most of this restriction, I asked the waiter if they had tall boys. Karen Marie laughed. The waiter didn't. I ordered a Miller Lite, as did she, and we talked nonstop until the pizza arrived. Conversation flowed so much easier this time. Maybe because we were face to face. The night before we sat side by side the whole time—in the car and at the movies, which made for awkward back and forth. But sitting across from each other, looking into each other's eyes, we seamlessly jumped from one topic to the next: family, friends, football (the Patriots were about to go all the way), what to do in Nashville and Boston for fun, where we'd been on vacation . . . you name it.

At one point after the pizza had arrived there was a lull and Karen Marie blurted out, "So, how's your sausage?"

I smirked.

She turned beet red and quickly followed up with "*Pizza,* your sausage *pizza!*"

She said if I wanted another beer she wouldn't tell.

The next evening Doc came by to check on me and get the details. I told him we had fun and I thought she was sweet but I didn't see where this was going, seeing we lived so far apart. He reiterated that it was still nice to have a friend in Nashville and then outlined what needed to be done in my next procedure.

"Then will I be done?" I asked him.

"Yes, if all goes well."

On my last night, Karen Marie and I were going to have dinner at the P. F. Chang's that had opened up near my hotel. Unfortunately two of my suture lines had also opened up, and Doc had to come over to do some emergency stitching. He told me I wouldn't be going anywhere. I called Karen Marie to break our date and let her know it was only because I was literally coming apart at the seams. The disappointment in her voice was surprising. And encouraging.

"Can I take a rain check?" I asked. "I have to come back for another procedure this spring."

"When?"

"Ah, I don't know yet. But I do know when I'm *not* coming."

She paused. "When?"

"When you're in New York."

••

I fell hard for Karen Marie. I knew she had just gotten out of a serious relationship and that there was a chance that I was just a "rebound," but she was like a drug, and I was addicted. When I wasn't making trips to Nashville and she wasn't in Boston or New York, we were on the phone for hours at a time. I loved the sound of her voice. She could tell me I was the biggest asshole in the world and her Southern drawl would make it sound sweet. I found the way she said, "I'm in the bed" instead of "I'm in bed" endearing.

And speaking of *in the bed* . . . five years and thirteen surgeries since Lucy, I had grown comfortable with my lower body. So when

Karen Marie suggested we jump in the shower together, this time I didn't wear swim trunks.

When I finally got the green light from Doc that it was safe to try out my new implant, we planned a special weekend together. I was told all I had to do was squeeze the small pump located inside my newly formed scrotum three or four times and I would be standing at attention and ready for action.

Right.

Best-laid, or rather *not*-laid plans.

I learned something new about being a man: how it feels when you can't get it up.

This was even more upsetting for me because I had gone through almost three years of pain and suffering to get to this very moment and it was supposed to be foolproof. The good news was I had some sensation down there and was able to have an orgasm despite Mr. Limpy.

I called Doc the next day and told him what happened. He subjected me to a battery of humiliating questions and then asked me to pump up the implant and email him a photo.

"Do they have windsocks in Greece?" I asked him. "Picture one on a day with no breeze."

By the time I went back to Nashville and got the implant issue "straightened out," it was too late. I flew back up north, knowing my roller-coaster relationship with Karen Marie was headed south. One day we were talking about marriage and her moving to Boston. The next day she would shut me out or pick a fight. When we saw each other again I knew nothing physical was going to happen; I could tell she didn't feel the same way about me anymore and worried that I really was just a rebound. I was right. The break-up call came the following week while I was in LA on a shoot. She said it was the timing: She wasn't ready for a serious relationship and all the travel that came with a long-distance one. She needed space. I, of course, took that to mean I still had a chance. That someday we'd get back together.

My hope was renewed months later when I received a large envelope from her in the mail. Inside was a glossy twelve-month photo calendar featuring the Nashville Bikini Team, a group I didn't know existed. I opened it up to March, where the yellow Post-It had directed me, and there she was, posed provocatively in a white string bikini. She signed it "Missing you in Nashville." That had to mean something, right? I called to thank her and told her she looked amazing. She told me she was coming to Boston for a conference in a few weeks and asked if I wanted a visitor. I said absolutely. I thought we were finally getting back together.

I was wrong.

I'd go back to Nashville for a few more procedures and we'd merely exchange pleasantries. Later I'd find out she was dating a member of the Tennessee Titans. My buddies would ask me which player. I'd tell them the kicker. They'd tell me that didn't count.

Sometimes guys do know just what to say.

It took me a long time to get over Karen Marie. I eventually came to realize we weren't right for each other, but at the time I was blinded by love and the desire to have what both my sisters and all of my closest friends already had: a soul mate.

I was also blinded by something else: the belief that things happen for a reason. I always wondered why God made me transgender. Out of all the people in the world, why me? I'm a good person. Why would he put me through such emotional agony? Lead me down a path so full of pain and suffering? The reason I came up with was that path led me to Karen Marie. I would've never met her had it not been for the surgery and this one-of-a-kind doctor in Nashville, of all places. I believed we were destined to be together, and that belief made everything make sense and justified all the hell I went through: She was the prize. Looking back, it was easier for me to hold on to her than let go of my entire belief system.

I still believe things happen for a reason, but I also believe reason can be a moving target, especially when it comes to love.

THE DATING GAME

2007–2009

As I handed her the small turquoise box, I couldn't help but commend myself on what a brilliant gift idea this was. The Elsa Peretti design inspired by the very places in Spain we'd just been. She untied the perfectly knotted white satin bow, removed the sterling silver necklace, and held it out in front of her face, quickly giving it the once-over.

"Reason for return?" she asked.

"She treats me like crap and doesn't deserve it."

Yes, I should've known dating my trainer would not end well. I had seen all the red flags but chose to ignore them. It was summer, she was hot, and I was dying to try out my new penis. Once again, I never got the chance. But I did learn two things: Never think with your dick, and don't buy birthday gifts for new girlfriends way in advance.

With our break-up now official and zero prospects on the horizon, I did what lots of single people in their late thirties do: Open a Match.com account. Or more specifically, I *re*opened the account I already had. Yes, I'd been on Match before. Perhaps you went out with me—Adguy111? At first I had been hesitant about the whole online dating thing, because I was worried about dating girls who didn't know my gender history. At what point do you spring that on somebody? In the end, it was irrelevant because unlike my two good friends who both found their husbands on Match, all I ended up with was a string of bad dates and a dent in my bank account. At least the stories proved to be entertaining. Client meetings often began with requests to hear about my latest blind-date debacle.

Since then, I'd learned from my mistakes and figured out how to read between the lines when evaluating member profiles. It's easy when you know the one rule of thumb: People lie. It's not malicious or anything. Everyone just wants to put their best foot forward. They think: *If they just meet me, they'll see how awesome I am and won't care that I lied about my age, posted photos of myself that are totally outdated, or checked the "on occasion" box when I'm really a full-blown chain-smoker.*

I didn't lie. I didn't include anything about my gender history because that's what it was: history. Something I would share with a woman when the time was right—certainly not before the first date. I was a man. A witty, successful, reasonably good-looking man who, after a few weeks, was still not getting any hits. When I complained about this to my sisters, they pulled up my profile for inspection.

"Shtine, you put yourself down as 5' 4"?" Wendy accused.

"I am," I said defensively, "with shoes on."

"You can't put that. Say you're 5' 8"."

"What? I'm not gonna lie."

"You have to or girls will keep ruling out your profile."

"And what do I do when I show up for the date? Stand on a chair the whole time?"

"Well, you're only gonna go out with girls shorter than you anyway, so they won't really know how tall you are."

I turned to my other sister. "Jill?"

"I agree with you, Shtine. You can't say you're 5' 8". Say you're 5' 6"—that's more believable."

"What? Come on, it's not like I'm 5' 2"."

"But they think you are," Wendy clarified.

"What?"

I was exhausting my older sister's patience. She took a deep breath and spoke slowly as though I were a child. "Shtine, girls always assume

guys lie about their height by two inches. So if you put down 5' 4",
they'll think you're really 5' 2". Get it?"

Again I looked to Jill. She nodded. "It's true, so actually if you don't
want to lie, then definitely say 5' 6", because then they'll think you're
5' 4", which you are."

My brain was now hurting. Not sure what to believe, I decided to
just leave my profile the way it was. Until the following evening when
I was home watching TV. I was having my way with the remote when
I landed on one of those CSI shows. I'd never actually watched one
before, but for whatever reason I decided to let the episode play out.
The murder suspect had left his wallet behind at the crime scene and the
cop was studying the driver's license found inside. The dialogue went
something like this:

Male Cop:	Well, at least we can put out a visual description: black hair, blue eyes, 5' 10".
Female Cop:	You mean 5' 8".
Male Cop:	Ah, no it says 5' 10" right here on his license.
Female Cop:	Everybody knows guys add two inches to their height. Trust me, he's 5' 8".

My jaw hit the floor. I grabbed my laptop and immediately changed
the height on my profile to 5' 6". Sure enough, the hits started coming.

That's how I ended up with "Gabby414" on a lunch date, which
quickly devolved into small talk of the we-have-no-chemistry-so-let's-
just-get-through-this variety.

"So, you're in advertising," Gabby said. "Have you done any com-
mercials I would've seen?"

"Did you ever see the McDonald's spot with the YouTube footage of
two guys rapping about McNuggets?"[6]

"I don't think so."

---

6   https://vimeo.com/45138580

"I'm into nuggets, y'all?"

Blank stare.

"McNuggets McNuggets rock?"

"I didn't see it."

"Okay, um . . ."

"What agency do you work for?"

"Arnold."

"Oh, I have a friend who used to work at Arnold—a long time ago though."

"I've been there fifteen years," I said. "What's her name? Maybe I know her."

I didn't.

"Well"—she leaned in—"you must've been there during the big scandal with the CEO. My friend told me all about it."

Hmmm . . . I didn't recall my father being in the middle of any scandals.

"What scandal?"

"The one about the CEO's daughter."

My thoughts immediately jumped to Jill, who also worked at Arnold at the time. But as far as I knew she wasn't involved in any scandals either. I had no idea what Gabby was talking about. I just shook my head and looked at her blankly.

She was stunned that I could be so clueless. "Ed Eskandarian. He's the CEO, right?"

"Yeah . . ."

"You know . . . how his daughter became his son—or was it his son who became his daughter? I don't remember. Which was it?"

Ho-ly shit. Is this really happening to me right now?

I could've let it go and played dumb, maybe even joined in on the gossip with her to find out what she'd heard. I didn't plan to go out with her again, so it's not like she'd find out I was being dishonest. But I'd come too far to be ashamed of who I was or what I'd been through. *Fuck it.*

"You tell me, you're lookin' at him."

"What?" She stared at me, confused.

"I said, 'You're look-ing at him.'"

The smile and color disappeared from her face.

"No."

"Yes."

"No."

"Yes."

"Don't tease me," she said. "It's not funny."

"I'm not teasing you."

"But your last name is different."

"I changed it."

"Oh my god, I'm so embarrassed."

"Don't be. I take it as a compliment you're so surprised."

Was it impolite of me to make her uncomfortable? Maybe. But was it stupid of her to be gossiping like that on a blind date? Definitely. The CEO's daughter could have been a good friend of mine. Either way, I decided to make it a teachable moment and told her a little bit about my background and how I transitioned on the job. I was a perfect gentleman to the end, paying for her lunch and holding the door for her on the way out. I wanted to ensure as much as I could that she had nothing negative to say about me when she inevitably relayed this story to her friends and family. If anyone was going to look bad, it was going to be her, not me.

My lunch with Gabby marked the end of my foray into online dating. Instead I decided to take a shot at meeting a girl the old-fashioned way: at a bar. Actually, my friend Hazel talked me into it. Her husband, Billy, was going to some CrossFit party and dragging her along, so she figured she'd drag me too. "Who knows," she said. "You might meet someone."

At the time, all I knew about CrossFit was that it was a new, primal workout concept and Hazel's husband was into it. He'd go to some pseudo-gym somewhere and throw tires over his head as many times as he could. The idea seemed crazy and dangerous to me, but perfectly logical to Billy, who made a habit of jogging up the steps of Harvard stadium wearing a backpack filled with bricks.

The party was upstairs at an Irish pub called Sólás. Most of the female attendees could squash me like a bug. Plus everyone seemed pretty young. While Billy socialized with his fellow tire-throwers, Hazel and I cased the joint.

"See anyone of interest?" she asked. As far as I was concerned there was only one cute girl in the entire room and she was standing over by the bar with two of her girlfriends, looking as out of place as I felt. Aside from Hazel, she was also the only female at the party with any modicum of style and . . . she just caught me staring at her. Crap. Well, at least she smiled.

"Long, brown, curlyish hair, blue sweater. Over by the bar at one o'clock."

Hazel nonchalantly looked over her shoulder. "Oh, she is cute. Let's grab Billy and go over there."

Why not? I had nothing to lose but my dignity. I'd never hit on a girl at a bar before, but there was a first time for everything. I finished my drink so I'd have an excuse to get another one and headed over to the bar with my two wingmen. Billy initiated contact.

"Do you guys go to CrossFit?" he asked.

They immediately said no.

"Thank God," I said. "I thought I was the only normal one here."

They laughed.

We all chatted for a bit and then my wingmen made a graceful exit. I introduced myself to Blue Sweater and discovered that her name was Jamie, she had a great sense of humor, and liked pizza as much as I did. She and her friends swore Santarpio's in East Boston was the best. I told them I'd heard that but had never been. After another hour or so Hazel and Billy were ready to go and so was I. It was after eleven and I'd had a long day at work. My pillow was calling, but seeing that it was Friday night, I told the girls I was on my way to another party so I wouldn't seem like a loser. They looked genuinely disappointed and kept harassing me to stay. *Leave them wanting more.*

I suggested we hit Santarpio's sometime and asked Jamie for her number. She watched me type it into my phone. I told her if I called it and got a towing company or something she'd be in big trouble. She assured me that wouldn't happen. I left in a great mood.

"I got digits," I announced in the car.

"Awesome! Now don't blow it." Hazel warned. "It's Friday, so wait 'til Tuesday to call her."

"Okay, okay."

When Tuesday rolled around I punched J for Jamie into my phone and hit send. I got her voicemail. *This is Jamie, leave a message and I'll call you back.* I decided to keep my message short and sweet—this was no time for improv: *Hey Jamie, it's Chris Edwards. We met at the party at Sólás the other night. Wondering if you want to grab a pizza at Santarpio's this weekend so I can see what all the fuss is about. Give me a call.*

I left my number clearly and twice, so there would be no confusion.

The next afternoon still no call back. I called Hazel.

"Is it possible I wasn't as charming as I thought I was?"

"No. It totally seemed like she was interested. She must be away or something. She'll call."

Thursday came and went. Still nothing. Friday nothing. The weekend went by and I found myself obsessing over every detail of that night and the message I left. I just couldn't understand why this girl would not call me back. I recounted the sequence of events to friends and coworkers, looking for answers. I got a bunch:

She's playing hard to get.

She really wasn't interested.

Maybe she has a boyfriend and was just flirting.

She deleted your voicemail by mistake, doesn't have your number, and is waiting for you to call her again.

Okay, that last one—that was possible. I'll call her again. What's the worst that could happen?

I closed my office door and pulled out my cell phone. Again I punched in J for Jamie but this time I noticed something. There were two Jamies in my contact list. Who the hell was the other Jamie? And more importantly, which one had I called? I didn't recognize either number. I called the first one and got the same voicemail as before. Was that her? I didn't recognize the voice as anyone else's. I called the second one.

"Hi, this is Jamie."

Shit! It was her. I should've thought this through.

"Heeeey, Jamie, it's . . . uh . . . Chris Edwards. I met you at that party at Sólás . . ."

Silence. Then, "Oh, yeah . . . Hi."

She's pissed.

"Yeah, so I tried calling you last week and left a message.".

"I never got it."

"I know . . . well, because, see, I was wondering why you never called me back, so today I was gonna try calling you again and I noticed there were two Jamies in my contact list. I must have asked out the other one."

Silence.

"She didn't call me back either."

Crickets.

Crap. I thought that would make her laugh.

"I don't even know who she is."

Oh my god, what am I saying? Stop talking. Stop talking.

Oh, but I didn't stop. And with each word I was becoming a bigger and bigger asshole. I blew it.

A couple days later I was waiting for the elevator on my floor and a junior creative, who was once my assistant for like five minutes, walked past me on her way to the ladies' room. I called after her.

"Hey, Jamie."

She backtracked a few steps. "Yeah?"

"Did I leave you a message asking you out a few weeks ago?"

"Yeah. You did."

"Why didn't you tell me I called the wrong person?"

"I thought you'd figure it out for yourself."

Yep, still just as helpful as she was as my assistant.

The Tale of Two Jamies led to another dry spell, so I let a coworker talk me into signing up for Table For Eight, a group-dating service that organizes four-on-four dinner parties. They're supposed to increase your odds of success and make the first date experience less awkward. Dinner guests are hand-selected based on compatibility and extensive in-depth membership profiles—at least that's what I was told.

My first group date was at an upscale restaurant in the Back Bay. The reservation was at 7:00 p.m., and at 7:05 I walked in appropriately attired in dark jeans, wing tips, and a sport coat. I approached the host's podium, not quite sure how to announce myself.

"Edwards, table for eight?" I whispered as though it were a secret password.

"Yes, sir. Go on upstairs. They're already seated."

"Everybody's here already?"

He nodded, adding with a hint of sympathy, "Good luck."

When I got to the top of the stairs, a hostess escorted me to a round table, where seven nerdy professionals sat awkwardly, trying to find common ground. The four women seemed older than the preferred age range I'd put down in my profile, and I wasn't physically attracted to any of them. I gathered the feeling was mutual; they couldn't have looked more disappointed to see me if they'd tried. I, however, was used to disappointment, so I didn't let it faze me. I put on a happy face and decided to make the best of it. I walked over to the only available chair and cheerfully addressed the group.

"Looks like I make eight."

They all ignored me.

I sat down and introduced myself to the woman on my right and the guy on my left. They both said hi, but didn't tell me their names. It was then I noticed everyone already had drinks. *Jesus, what time did they all get here?* While I waited for my vodka soda to arrive, I sat listening to the painful small talk from which I was being excluded. "Ted" from Rhode Island had taken a car, a bus, and a cab to get to this place and couldn't believe how long it took. The woman sitting directly across from me began playing the role of conversation generator, lobbing out topics for discussion every few minutes. I was guessing she had a cheat sheet up her sleeve. I couldn't take it anymore.

"Hi, sorry to interrupt, I know I was five minutes late and you all might have covered this already, but could we go around the table and everyone say their name and what they do?"

Lawyer, engineer, chemist, pediatrician, teacher, researcher, neurosurgeon, ad guy. Which one of these things doesn't belong? It was like getting stuck at the mish-mosh singles table at a wedding you didn't want to attend in the first place.

Since I was the only one who appeared to have any social skills, I spent the first half-hour asking a lot of questions and facilitating conversation organically. I got one-word answers that went nowhere. Well, except when I asked the teacher what she'd be doing with her summer off. She said she was going to teach summer school part-time and also do some nannying.

Since my sister Jill was looking for a nanny, I followed up with, "Oh, do you have a family—"

"ISN'T THAT WHY WE'RE ALL HERE?" she barked.

The table fell silent. I finished my sentence.

"—to nanny for?"

After that I gave up and just kept drinking. When I wasn't texting friends from the men's room, I was back at the table, fruitlessly injecting myself into conversations. The pediatrician/topic lobber was talking about how she had to catch a flight the next morning. Seeing that I had just flown, I chimed in.

"I just flew back from Chicago yesterday. I had a window seat, which I hate. I always like to be on the aisle because I always have to pee. Same thing when I'm at the movies."

I figured this might prompt a group debate on which is better: aisle or window? Or how it sucks to have to pee in the middle of a good movie. But the pediatrician took a different tack.

"How many times could you possibly have to go to the bathroom during a movie?" she said.

"I don't know, once . . . twice maybe. Depends on how much I've had to drink beforehand."

"You DRINK before you go to the movies?"

"Well, I usually have some type of beverage with my DINNER, which I often go out to before a movie."

Just in time, the waiter came over to clear the plates. "Would anyone like dessert?" he asked.

"NO," I shouted involuntarily. But Ted had come a long way and he wasn't leaving without trying the bananas foster.

Somebody kill me.

By my thirty-ninth birthday, despite all my attempts, I was still single. I wondered then, as I often did, what my life would be like had I been born a biological male—the way I was supposed to be. I'd probably be married, maybe even have kids. I would've been considered a catch. If I'd had this much trouble finding someone, more of my friends and family would have certainly tried to fix me up. All those times in my late twenties hearing them talk about how they needed to find someone for so and so, I was almost never in the running. I understood why; I mean, when it came to baggage, I was toting around one big-ass carry-on.

But being ruled out still hurt. And now, I was worried I'd missed my window of opportunity. I began to let resentment creep in. *After all I do for everyone else, nobody was helping me.* Granted, I never asked for help. I'm not good at that. But even if I did, most of my friends were now married, having kids, and living in the suburbs. Fixing me up wasn't at the top of their to-do list. Even if it was, how many single girls did they know? As I became more vocal about my dismay, people began trying. I went on a few blind dates but none of them worked out, mainly because the matchmakers were asking themselves, "Who do I know that's single?" not, "Who do I know that's single and a great match for Chris?"

I was feeling helpless and needed a way to take back control. So I decided to take myself out of the game for a while. They say relationships happen when you're not looking. I was hoping "they" were right.

THE 40-YEAR-OLD VIRGIN

May 18, 2009

When I turned forty, my family threw me a blowout at Foley's Pub in the South End. One hundred of my closest friends were there to celebrate with me. It was like the wedding I never had.

My former creative partner Mike and his wife, Lisa, even flew in from Atlanta and presented me with a bottle of Dom Perignon before the party. It was a generous gift and I was excited to save it for a special occasion, which Mike assumed was now.

"Let's pop this sucker open," he said. "Where do you keep your glasses?"

Lisa was glaring at him. "Ah, Mike, that's a gift for Chris, not for you. Maybe he'd like to save it for a special occasion."

Mike turned to me. "Now is special. You're fucking forty, dude."

"Yeah, but I'm gonna be drinking vodka all night. I'd rather save it."

"For what?"

"Mike!" Lisa chastised. "Sorry, Chris, can you tell he's dying to try it?"

"I've never had it," Mike whined.

"Well, now I know what to get you when *you* turn forty," I said.

"Chris, you should save it," Lisa said, shutting her husband down.

"I know, I'll save it for when I finally get to try out my penis!"

Mike rolled his eyes. "Does champagne go bad, Lisa?"

"Ha, ha," I said, swiping the bottle from his hand.

He kept going. "Make sure you store it on its side, Chris—after a few years the cork dries out."

●●

The first few months after my party I did feel an urgency to have sex—not so I could break open the Dom, but to make sure my new penis actually worked. It cost a shitload of money, years of pain and suffering, and had been ready for action shortly after my "failure to launch" incident of 2005—coincidentally the same year *The 40-Year-Old Virgin* came out. With my forty-first birthday now looming on the horizon, I did not want to be inspiration for the sequel.

I had already learned that due to my unique situation, a one-night stand wasn't a realistic option for me. I had flown to New York City to look at rough cuts the creative teams had been working on. Dinner that night was at Gaslight, a French restaurant across the street from the Hotel Gansevoort, where everyone but me was staying. The director showed up with a friend—"Candice"—whom I talked with quite a bit during cocktails. She was a natural beauty, a free spirit, and only back in town for a few days before jetting off to Amsterdam. We got separated during dinner at opposite ends of the long table. I was stuck sitting next to the director who appeared to be on coke. He kept disappearing to the men's room, each time returning to the table more jittery and more obnoxious. The female creative across from me bore the brunt of his behavior and after he spilled a drink on her, she got up and left. Within seconds Candice filled her empty seat. She and I continued chatting, and after another round of drinks we all trickled outside the restaurant to say our goodbyes. Candice asked me if I was staying at the Gansevoort. I told her they were booked so I was staying at the Carlton in midtown. She said her place was just a few blocks away and a lot nicer than the Carlton. Before I could respond, my dutiful producer grabbed me and threw me into the cab he'd managed to flag down, then slammed the door behind me. I sat there in shock, watching the group disperse and Candice walk away.

I was still processing what might have been when the cab driver interrupted me.

"Where you going?"

"See that girl in the navy jacket?"

"Yeah."

"I could've been going home with her. But instead I'm going to the Carlton on Madison."

On the rainy ride into midtown I replayed the situation in my head and decided my producer probably saved me from embarrassment. I mean, let's say I did go home with Candice. Would I have to tell her about my surgery? If I didn't, would she be able to tell the difference? And what if my penis didn't work? How would I explain that? It hit me then that I would most likely never know what it feels like to have a one-night stand. Not that I was that type anyway, but still, it made me a bit sad to know the option was off the table; just one more reminder that I would never be a "regular" guy.

I relayed this story to my brothers-in-law over a few beers. They both told me I needed to relax and be patient.

"It's been FOUR YEARS," I snapped.

"Shtine, if it's that big a deal, my offer still stands," Lane said.

I looked at him and just shook my head.

"What offer?" Mike asked.

I sighed. "Lane offered to get me a hooker for my birthday."

"Not a hooker, Shtiny," Lane interjected. "A high-class call girl."

Mike laughed. "Actually, it's not a bad idea, I'll chip in."

"Are you two insane?"

Lane went into sales mode. "Think about it, Shtine. You're so anxious about it working or not, you might as well try it out on someone you'll never have to see again. Then if it doesn't work, who cares?"

"Lane's got a point, Shtine," Mike said. "You could get some practice in so when you finally get the GF, you'll know what you're doing."

"I'm not paying for sex," I said.

"You won't be," Mike said, laughing. "We will."

I rolled my eyes. I admit I actually considered it for a second. Then I just felt dirty. Nope. I wanted my first time to be with someone I really cared about—who cared about me. So I decided if I was ever going to have sex, it would be when I was in a meaningful relationship. But God only knew when that would be.

With my love life in the toilet, I focused on my work. I earned an Executive Vice President title and accomplished all the goals I'd laid out for myself when I accepted the position on McDonald's. It had taken seven years instead of five, but I'd done it. My team's work was on the agency sizzle reel and showcased in new business pitches. Creatives were now asking to work on my account, and talented creative directors were helping me run it. Awards were rolling in. And our little spot about a singing fish was making a big splash.[7]

We knew we had something memorable when we were shooting the spot and couldn't get the damn song out of our heads: *Give me back that Filet-O-Fish, give me that fiiiish.* Talk about an earworm. But the reaction we got after the spot aired was something we never could have predicted. In just three hours it went viral, spawning ring tones, DJ remixes, multiple fan clubs on Facebook, and by the end of its twenty-eight-day run, over a million hits on YouTube. Then came the local, regional, and national press. The hype was crazy and my clients were ecstatic, especially when their numbers came in. Filet-O-Fish sales were through the roof. And like the sandwich, we were on a roll (well, technically, a steamed bun). For the first time in history, McDonald's green-lighted a sequel and toy that sang the original version of the hit song as well as a club remix. (If you're interested, there might be a few still available on Amazon.)

I was flying high . . . and putting in sixty- to seventy-hour weeks. The projects just kept coming. I expected a lot from my team and ran

---

7   https://vimeo.com/46715720

the Mickey D's account with a "work hard, play hard" philosophy. I organized all sorts of social events to keep everyone motivated—from lunches and post-work cocktails to my infamous roof-deck parties and the ever-popular "Sox in the Box" night in Arnold's skybox at Fenway Park. So it was only natural I found myself spending a lot more time with another creative director in my group, both inside and outside the office. And I didn't mind one bit.

Mary was the whole package: beautiful, talented, witty, and stylish (with extra points for being shorter than me). She didn't know it, but I'd had a crush on her way back when she first started as an art director at Arnold. She had won a bunch of awards at another agency, so her creative reputation preceded her. I was attracted to her immediately, and since the printer I used was right outside her office, I began printing out my scripts one page at a time. In regular, six-minute intervals.

Back then, she was already in a serious relationship and assigned to different accounts than I was, so our paths never really crossed. Ten years later, here she was in my group and available. Technically, however, I was her boss, so I kept things professional at first, which was initially easy as she wasn't sending me any vibes that she'd be interested in anything more than a working relationship. I remember being on set once, posing for a picture with the rest of the creatives. Mary happened to be standing next to me, so I casually put my arm around her shoulder—like you do for group pictures—and she immediately stiffened like a board. I assumed I'd crossed a line. But a few months later while on another shoot, she specifically asked someone to take a picture of just the two of us and rested her head on my shoulder. *Hmmmm* . . .

The flirting went on for weeks but I was still getting mixed signals. She'd been talking about wanting to see the movie *The Hurt Locker* because it won so many awards. I asked her if she wanted to go. She turned me down. Flat out. No excuses. The next day she asked me if I still wanted to see it. *(Yes.)* She said it was only on On-Demand, so we'd have to watch it at my place. *(Interesting.)* I'd upped the ante and suggested dinner first, so there we were, getting to know each other over adobo steak and a bottle of Malbec.

"I can't believe I'm on a date with you," she said after a few sips of wine.

"Okay, so this *is* a date then?" I asked. I had chosen a quaint Venezuelan restaurant because it was a fun spot to go with a friend but could also double as a romantic place to bring a date. Since I didn't know what exactly "this" was, I figured I'd hedge my bets.

She smiled, blushing. "Well, I was hoping it was."

"Good. Me too."

I asked Mary if she was aware of my "background." She said yes and that it didn't matter to her. She only knew me as a guy and that's how she thought of me. I remember thinking she was too good to be true.

She held my hand on the walk home. It felt comfortable. Right. This woman was someone I could see a future with. I knew that soon she'd be leaving for a two-week vacation in Bali, so when we got back to my place, I presented her with a care package I'd made her for the trip. No, it did not include a mix tape. It was a mix CD. And I think it was the clincher. We never got to the movie.

We spent all our free time together until she left for her trip. That morning, after I dropped her off at the airport, I just couldn't get her out of my mind. On my way to work I kept worrying: What if something happens to her on one of the legs of her nineteen-hour journey? I was about four blocks from my house when I pulled out my phone and dialed her number.

Hey, it's me. I know you're on the plane and can't pick up but I wanted to leave you a message and tell you that I . . . I think I'm falling in love with you. I just wanted to make sure you knew that.

I didn't know I'd fall so deeply in love with Mary. That she would love me back so completely and unconditionally. That we'd be together for years. That our relationship would take me to places I'd never expected—like Ireland, Austria, and a remote part of Mexico where I would get fleas. That I'd find myself attending falconry school, releasing baby sea turtles into the ocean, snuggling with an Italian Greyhound named Finn, or kayaking for so long I'd end up offering a few houseboaters a thousand bucks for a six-pack and a tow. At the time I didn't know any of that. All I knew was that I had an important email to send out.

To: Mike; Lisa

Subject: It works

Date: April 3, 2010 10:40:38 AM EDT

From: Chris Edwards

EPILOGUE

July 28, 2014

"So, Shtine, what's the latest with the book? Any updates?"

This was my cue. The answer to Wendy's question would serve as the opening to a conversation with my nieces that had me filled with anxiety. They knew their Uncle Shtiny had written a book and were very curious what it was about. My previous answer, "It's about me," seemed to be enough to satisfy eight-year-old Ava, but not Calla, who at age eleven was full of questions. My sister and I figured if the girls hadn't already been exposed to the "T word," they would be soon, and we wanted to shape their impressions before anyone else did. So after some debate we decided the time to tell them was now, sitting at the kitchen table while the girls schooled me at a card game called "golf."

"Well, a bunch of editors are reading my book right now, and hopefully one of them will like it enough to publish it. Then maybe you girls will get to read it someday." They both smiled—especially Calla, who had just accomplished her goal of reading one hundred books in a year.

"So . . . do you guys know what my book is about?"

Calla nodded. "It's an autobiography, right?"

"Yes, kind of. It's actually called a *memoir*. The difference is an autobiography is about someone's entire life from start to finish. A memoir is about a certain time period or event in someone's life and focuses the story around that. You guys don't know this, but your Uncle Shtiny went through something very, very hard, and I wrote this book so I could help other people going through the same thing." I looked at Wendy and took a deep breath.

"When I was born, I had a girl's body."

Calla's big brown eyes went wide just for a second—as though she caught herself looking surprised and didn't want to hurt my feelings. Ava looked down at her lap and began shuffling the cards in her hands. *Keep it simple*, I reminded myself.

"But I knew I was a boy ever since I was four or five and couldn't understand why everyone thought I was a girl and why my body didn't match. I was really, really sad for a long, long time. I didn't think I could tell anyone or that anyone would understand. I was worried people would laugh at me or make fun of me. So I just kept my feelings inside and got sadder and sadder." Calla's eyes began to well up. I couldn't read Ava. She just kept her head down, avoiding eye contact.

"Finally I got the courage to tell Mimi and Popsie and your mom and Aunty GG. And they were supportive and helped me find the right doctors who could help me. And now that my body matches who I am, I'm so happy and everything's okay."

I paused and looked to Wendy for guidance. Her eyes had teared up too. So I changed my tone to be more upbeat. "I'm still the same Uncle Shtiny you know and love. This doesn't change who I am . . . I just wanted you to know who I *was*. And I didn't want you to find out by reading my book!" They both laughed.

Wendy chimed in and explained how this was different from being gay, which was great because she knows better than I do what they already know and understand about sexuality. Then I told them the word used to describe this is "transgender," and that they will probably be hearing the term a lot in school and on the news. I thought this was important because with kids now transitioning at all ages, schools at every level were reevaluating and in many cases evolving their policies to be more inclusive of transgender students. I told the girls there might be kids in their class who were going through what I went through, and that I hoped they'd be understanding and treat them like they would anyone else. I then made sure they knew this wasn't a secret about me; that everyone in our entire family knew except for Chase and Jake (my nephews). We didn't think they were old enough to understand so we weren't going to tell them yet.

Then we all kind of just sat there.

"Well . . . are you surprised?" I asked, breaking the tension.

They both smiled and nodded vigorously. They didn't have any questions but Wendy and I told them if they ever did, they should feel free to ask us.

And that was it. The card game continued. I lost as usual and it was like nothing had happened. The next day at the beach I caught Ava staring at my bare chest with a little extra scrutiny, but as soon as our eyes met she turned away quickly, grabbed her boogie board, and headed for the shoreline with her cousins who were still in the dark about my past. I confided to Wendy that I was worried my revelation would change the way the girls looked at me and, in turn, the close nature of our relationship. "Absolutely not," she said. "They love you, Shtine. I *am* surprised they haven't asked me any questions, though. I thought last night before bed they'd bring it up, but nuthin'."

The following day Calla did have a question for me.

"Am I in the book?"

••

If you'd asked me twenty years ago if I ever thought I'd write a book about my transition, I would've said hell no. I never wanted to be an activist or "poster boy" for the transgender movement. All I wanted was to get through my transition and put it behind me—live my life as a regular guy. It took time but I achieved that goal. I'm not my parents' transgender son. I'm their son. My friends don't introduce me as their "trans friend Chris." Just Chris (or "P-Head" or "Eddie" or "Bird"). And at Arnold, I wasn't Chris Edwards, the Transgender Creative Director. I was simply a creative director—well, an EVP/Group Creative Director. I don't want to sell myself short!

Thankfully, my story has a happy ending. But I'm one of the lucky ones. For the majority of the trans population, the picture isn't quite so rosy. This is especially true for transgender youth. The sad fact is fifty-one percent of all transgender teens will attempt suicide (compared to 7.8 percent of teens in the general population).[8] And without parental support, many of them will succeed. It took seventeen-year-old Leelah Alcorn to bring attention to this staggering statistic.[9] Her story, which made headlines and went viral on social media last year, opened up a national discussion about "fixing society" through gender education. Schools at all levels are now doing more and more to educate students on this topic and are adjusting their policies to be more inclusive of transgender kids. I believe this is critical as education and understanding will lead to acceptance. But all too often, as in Leelah's case, the problem isn't at school. It's at home.

While numbers are hard to quantify, studies suggest that nearly sixty percent of transgender teens go without support from their families, and in those cases the risk of suicide is much higher.[10] I know if I hadn't had the support of my family, I wouldn't be here today. That said, when I first told my mom and dad, they weren't all, "Well, let's go get you some surgery!" You may remember they initially asked me to reconsider. But their reaction was based on fear—fear that I would be deemed an outcast by society and lose all of my friends; that I would be worse off than I already was. But once I started coming out to my friends and my parents saw how amazingly supportive each and every one of them was, that's when they got fully on board. With this overwhelming acceptance, suddenly my future didn't look so bleak. They believed I had a chance at happiness and they were going to do whatever they could to increase my odds.

---

8   Statistics found at: http://www.nydailynews.com/life-style/health/1-12-teens-attempted-suicide-report-article-1.1092622.

9   For more on Leelah Alcorn's story, see: http://www.popsugar.com/tech/Teen-Leaves-Suicide-Note-Tumblr-36373960.

10   For more on parental support, see: http://www.academia.edu/7252800/Impacts_of_Strong_Parental_Support_for_Trans_Youth.

When you get right down to it, all parents really want is for their child to live a full and happy life. And for parents of kids who are transgender, gender education alone isn't going to provide that reassurance. What I think would really help is hearing more success stories from regular people who can show trans kids, their parents, and society as a whole that being transgender doesn't have to forever define you (unless you want it to). That you can still build a successful career, get married, raise a family— basically live a "normal" life just like everybody else. I believe those kinds of everyday success stories would give parents a more optimistic outlook for their child, which in turn would lead to greater parental support for trans kids overall and fewer suicide attempts. Not to mention it would also give the rest of the world a more complete picture of the transgender population.

The inherent problem with this solution is it means asking people who've purposely been avoiding the transgender spotlight to go center stage. That's a lot to ask. Which is why there aren't many of these stories to point to. All I can tell you is they do exist. I'm living proof.

Thanks to others who've come before me, the transgender topic is finally being talked about openly. My hope is that having read my story, you'll continue the conversation.

ACKNOWLEDGMENTS

To say I self-published this book, while technically true, wouldn't be accurate. It was a four-year uphill battle, and there were so many people along the way who helped put *BALLS* in your hands.

Jim Eber, the man of many metaphors, I learned so much from you about the editing process. You have the patience of a saint. Thank you for helping me "find the thread" and cut 27,000 precious words. More importantly, thank you for continually saving me from myself.

My former boss and longtime friend, **Pete Favat**, for giving me the idea to call the book *BALLS* during our vodka-fueled brainstorm at Baxter's and for bringing my vision for the cover to life. A thousand times thank you to you and your killer crew at Deutsch LA: **Nathan Iverson**, **Ali Ring**, **John Cluckie**, and **Katie "Nice Legs!" Dittman**.

Bob Mecoy for believing my story was one that needed to be told before it was fashionable to do so.

Alan Nevins for helping me even though I was way below your pay grade. We came so close! To you, I dedicate Whitney Houston's 1987 ballad, "Didn't We Almost Have it All."

Pieta Pemberton for recognizing there was a story worth telling in that 367-page mess of a first draft. Your guidance and championing of my story got me on the right path. Every time I have a slice of pie or see the number 3.14, I will think of you fondly.

The incredible **Marnie Cochran** for taking all my calls and emails, making calls and emails on my behalf, and checking in on me periodically to make sure I hadn't jumped off a ledge somewhere. Your honest, round-the-clock advice was invaluable to me. You were so generous with your time, your days must be 28 hours long. xoxo

Jeanne Emanuel for your relentless efforts in trying to get me published. Every time I was about to give up I'd get an email from you with another lead. You are truly one of a kind.

Professor **Sue Shapiro**, I wish I'd found you sooner. Taking your *Instant Gratification Takes Too Long* writing class was one of the best decisions I ever made.

Social media standout **Dorie Clark**, author of *Stand Out* (see what I did there?): Ten minutes after we met, you invited me to a dinner party at your house, and I stunned you by saying yes. Since then, you've become a mentor, a cheerleader, and a friend. I still suck at Twitter, but thanks to your RTs, I'm still picking up followers.

When I started this endeavor people said to me, "Oh you're in advertising, you *must* know tons of people in publishing." Ah, no. Two totally different fields. I had zero connections. So I'd like to thank my peers and other industry professionals who believed enough in my story to either help me personally or connect me with people who could (apologies to anyone I may have forgotten due to the time pressure of making this deadline): **Val DiFebo, Edward Boches, Bobby Orr, Margie Sullivan, Noreen Moross, Susan Titcomb, Suzy Marden, Loc Truong, Ali Pace, Jane Roper, Karen Alpert, Mark St. Amant, Jennifer Palmer, Lou Palmer, Alex Shumway, Chris Gayton, Tamra Blais, Alison Fargis, Steve Almond, Tess Johnson, Naomi Rosenblatt, Patty Stone, Lisa Price, Helayne Spivak, Merinda Salsky, Wendy Semonian, Nick Teich, Steph Hofmann, Marie-Claire Barker, Fei Wu, Deb Wojnarowski, Barb Reilly, Kel Kelly,** and **Laura Morton,** who single-handedly changed my trajectory.

My early draft readers (you know who you are), with a shout-out to the legendary **Ron Lawner**: Thanks so much for your feedback and the confirmation that my writing didn't suck. Your validation gave me the confidence to press on. Also, special props to **Holly Raynes**, author of *Nation of Enemies* and winner of the 1996 Arnold Lampshade award.

My heartfelt gratitude for red-lining multiple drafts and weighing in at all hours on countless excerpts ("Which is better A or B?").

My talented creative and technical panel for their continual support, advice and mad skills: **LD Belanger, Mike Martin, Alex Dobert, Maggie Keller, Sheila McKee, Lára Vukson, Nunzio, Anna Echiverri, Mary Beth Koeth, Bronac MacNeil, Lauren Bruck Simon, Kyle Megrath, Melissa MacNish, Ema Loftis,** and **Mo Norman.**

Grub Street for their annual **Muse and The Marketplace** conference. I highly recommend attending this event to any writer starting out on or in the middle of their journey.

Amy Blankenship and the gang at **Soundtrack** and **Finish Post** for hosting my Arnold going away party, renting me office space at rock bottom prices, and keeping the kitchen stocked with Caffeine-free Diet Coke and Peanut M&Ms.

The Boston Ad Club for giving me my first speaking gig and not yanking me off the stage when my time was up. **Swellen Wallett** for those endless hours of frame-fucking in the edit bay and the female to male adaptor story that, twenty years later, still gets good laughs.

Kat Gordon for making me a closer at The 3% Conference and exposing me to the most amazing group of women in the ad industry. Your continual support and encouragement means the world to me.

Francis Storrs at *The Boston Globe Magazine* for being the first to publish me and **David Griner** at *Adweek* for my first major interview about *BALLS*. **Bonnie Graham** and **Maggie Linton** for giving me radio experience, and **Judi** and **Jaime Guild** for landing me on *Chronicle*, my first (and hopefully not last) TV appearance.

Authors **David Sedaris, Augusten Burroughs, Mary Karr,** and **Lisa Genova** for inspiring me. **Laverne Cox** for your words of encouragement and support.

Bet MacArthur for saving my life and **"DS"** for saving my sanity. (I know, I know, *Rent is expensive up there!*)

The makers of **Ativan, Ambien, Grey Goose,** and **Stolichnaya.** And of course, **Fong** and her fucking spoon.

Doc, over the last fourteen years you've taught me more about being a man than I ever could have imagined. You're no longer my doctor; you're my friend who occasionally does surgery on me.

Special thanks to all the nurses and medical professionals who helped get me through 28 procedures with dignity, sensitivity, and TLC. Big hugs to **Karen Barker, Melinda, Elaine, Patti, Theresa, Jaime,** and **Bella**.

To my Loews Vanderbilt family: **Doug, Nina, Evelyn, Steve, Wadell, Igor, Marta, Faith**, and many others I can't remember by name. Thank you for going above and beyond to make my stays in Nashville as painless as possible.

To **my Arnold family** during the "Camelot" years, your acceptance and support was everything. **JP Smith**, I still have that Bar Mitzvah card!

Mickey, I simply would not have made it through my transition without you. You were always there supporting me through the lows and celebrating with me during the highs. Not only did I have you behind me, I had your entire family . . . and still do. That bond means so much to me.

My fellow Fab Fivers: **Melvin, Mare, Schu,** and **Meek**. You are my core. There is nobody else I laugh longer or harder with. Not many people are still tight with their friends from grade school, let alone after transitioning. Thank you for not letting my gender change change our dynamic. I treasure you guys.

My dear friend **Hazel**. The moment I heard you cackle from across the room when Professor Coyle called bullshit on my impromptu interpretation of Baudelaire, I knew we would end up friends. There are very few things in this world I'm sure of. You are one of them.

The Colgate Women's Rugby Team 1990–1994. You ho-bags know who you are. Special thanks to **Price** for listening, empathizing, and always coming through with a Shaw's cake – gold with buttercream frosting. It's really not that hard, **Fedin**.

My Greenleaf Team: **Justin, Emilie, Lindsey, Liz, Neil, Carrie, Sheila, Brittany, Corrin,** and **Steve**. Thank you all for handling

BALLS with care. The "I survived Mr. Type A⁺" bumper stickers are on the way!

My Sunshine Sachs trifecta: **Nina**, **Karissa**, and **Janell**. Here's hoping I won't ever need to enlist your crisis management skills!

My Facebook friends and Twitter followers: You may number in the hundreds not the thousands, but I believe in quality not quantity! Your support keeps me going.

Mary, thank you for taking a chance on me. I wouldn't trade our three and a half years together for anything.

And last but not least, **my unbelievable family**, including my extended family of "Armos" and the *odars* who married in. Thank you all for accepting me as I am and never once treating me any differently.

Gram, I think of you every day. I hope Amazon delivers to heaven (and that the shipping is covered by my *Prime* membership).

Mom and Dad, you always put my happiness first—even when it scared the crap out of you. I wouldn't be the man I am today without your love and support. Thank you for instilling in me the importance of family and for being the best parents and role models I could ever ask for.

Weezer and **G**: They say a sister is a little piece of childhood that can never be lost. I don't know who "they" are, but they got it right; I can't imagine "growing up Shtiny" without you guys. Thank you for having my back at every turn. I cherish you both.

Lane and **Mike**, my brothers-~~in-law~~.

Finally, to **Calla**, **Ava**, **Chase** and **Jake**: Thank you for making me feel 100% loved. I look at you kids and I see the generation where prejudice ends and acceptance truly begins.

RESOURCES

When I began my journey more than twenty years ago, there were very few places my family and I could turn to for information or guidance. Today, there are so many transgender resources out there, if I tried to gather them all and list them here, I would miss my publication date. Instead, I'll leave the googling to you, and single out the two organizations closest to my heart.

Camp Aranu'tiq

This amazing summer camp for transgender youth changes lives. Kids don't come here to learn about being transgender. They come here to make friends, have fun and just be themselves. There's no worrying about what anybody might think, or having to second-guess decisions like what to wear or what bathroom to use. These may seem like small things, but not when you hear directly from the campers about their experience and what a safe haven like this means to them. Having an extended support network outside the home does wonders for self-esteem, and knowing there are other kids like you out there can make all the difference in the world. The camp also hosts family long weekends that provide an opportunity for parents to meet other parents, share experiences and learn from one another. Find out more at camparanutiq.org.

PFLAG/Greater Boston PFLAG

The national Parents, Families, and Friends of Lesbians and Gays (PFLAG) organization and its chapters are a great resource for families, friends, and anyone looking for ways to become an ally to someone they know who is LGBTQ. When it comes to the "T," Greater Boston PFLAG has the most expansive and well-organized set of resources, supports, and programs for parents and caregivers of trans people in the state. They've also been doing a ton of work to educate schools and corporations big and small on what being transgender means and how to foster safe and inclusive environments for students and employees. And when it comes to advocating for transgender rights, they are out there on the front lines. For more information, check out gbpflag.org. To find your local chapter, visit PFLAG's national website at pflag.org.

ABOUT THE AUTHOR

Chris Edwards grew up in the Boston suburbs and was voted Most Likely to Get an Ulcer by his high school classmates. He went on to attend Colgate University, where he majored in psychology and minored in keg stands. After building an award-winning advertising career spanning nearly 20 years, Chris left his post as EVP, Group Creative Director at Arnold Worldwide to write his memoir, *BALLS*. Since then he's become a sought-after speaker, inspiring audiences with his courageous story and compelling message that we actually have the power to control how others define us.

He has yet to develop an ulcer.

For more on Chris including speaking engagements, book signings and press, go to chrisedwardsballs.com. For more on his advertising career and creative work, check out chrisedwardscreative.com.